THE ESSENTIAL

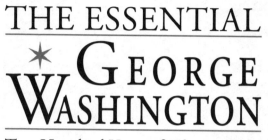

GEORGE WASHINGTON

Two Hundred Years of Observations
On the Man, the Myth, the Patriot

Washington life mask, by Houdon.

THE ESSENTIAL

GEORGE WASHINGTON

Two Hundred Years of Observations On the Man, the Myth, the Patriot

Compiled and edited by

Peter Hannaford

Images from the Past, Inc.
Bennington, Vermont

Cover: Life mask of Washington by French sculptor
Jean Antoine Houdon

1 2 3 4 5 6 7 8 9 10 XXX 06 05 04 03 02 01 00 99

Library of Congress Cataloging-in-Publication Data
The Essential George Washington: two hundred years of observations on the
man, the myth, the patriot/compiled and edited by Peter Hannaford.

    p. cm.
    Includes bibliographical references and index.
    ISBN 1-884592-23-6
    1. Washington, George, 1732-1799—anecdotes. 2. Presidents—
United States—Biography—Anecdotes. I. Hannaford, Peter.

    E312 .15 .E67 1999
    973.4'1 092-dc21
    [B]

                                    99-045056

Copyright© 1999 Peter Hannaford
Published by Images from the Past, Inc.,
P.O. Box 137, Bennington, VT 05201
Tordis Ilg Isselhardt, Publisher

Printed in the United States of America

Design and Production: Ron Toelke Associates, Chatham, NY
Printer: Thomson-Shore, Inc., Dexter, MI

Dedicated to the women of the
Mount Vernon Ladies' Association,
who saved Washington's home
for posterity, and who have
worked tirelessly to make
his life relevant to each
passing generation.

TABLE OF

PART I: VOICES OF A YOUNG NATION

CONTENTS

PREFACE

This book is an album of verbal "snapshots" of George Washington and his world as seen by his contemporaries, by well-known figures of the nineteenth and early twentieth centuries, and by our own contemporaries. It is my hope that, taken together, these observations will give a full understanding of Washington, whose qualities were greatly admired in his day and for long afterward, but seem in very short supply in our era of moral relativism.

The words of these contributors help us begin to understand George Washington and his world. As one delves into the written record of the day, Washington comes to life. The forces that shaped his character become apparent. He had a clear understanding of the difference between right and wrong, and he exhibited a highly developed sense of honor. He treated all people with respect. He refrained from attacking the motives of others, preferring instead to try to understand them. As president, he knew that people expected him to set a good example, and he conducted himself accordingly.

If he were here with those qualities today, he would make a good president for the twenty-first century.

Peter Hannaford
Washington, D.C.
July 1999

ACKNOWLEDGMENTS

My thanks go to the modern-day contributors of observations about George Washington and to a number of others who helped make this book possible:

My friend and former neighbor, Nancy Call, vice regent for California of the Mount Vernon Ladies' Association, who reawakened my interest in Washington. Mary Thompson, researcher at Mount Vernon, for her always cheerful and efficient responses to my inquiries. Jim Rees, resident director of Mount Vernon, for his early advice on how to approach Washington. Karlyn Bowman and her assistant Melissa Knauer at the American Enterprise Institute for sharing fifty years worth of polling data on American leaders. Jill Hays, for her diligent illustration research. Stuart Murray, friend and fellow author, who introduced me to my publisher, Tordis Isselhardt, and who served as project editor for the book. To Tordis, for her enthusiasm and keen appreciation of the relevance of major historical figures to today's world.

And, to my wife, Irene, whose love, support, and unerring transcription of taped interviews were essential ingredients in the project.

INTRODUCTION

It is no exaggeration to say that without George Washington there might never have been a United States of America. Washington was a genuine war hero. He embodied the unity of purpose of the founders at Philadelphia. As president, he got the fledgling government on its feet and kept it out of a European war. Historian James Thomas Flexner called Washington "The Indispensable Man"—indispensable to the formation and early sustenance of our republic.

Modern audiences have a more narrow perspective.

In May 1995, a Roper Center poll asked the question, "Over the past 200 years, of all of the United States presidents, which do you think did the best job?" The result placed Washington in a sixth-place tie with Theodore Roosevelt, behind Abraham Lincoln, John F. Kennedy, Franklin D. Roosevelt, Ronald Reagan, and Don't know/No answer. In the same poll, respondents were also asked, "Regardless of which president you think did the best job, of all the presidents, living or dead, with which one would you most want to have a conversation?" The Father of His Country was in a seventh-place tie with George Bush, and behind Kennedy, Lincoln, Bill Clinton, Reagan, and Richard Nixon and Jimmy Carter (tied).

The worst was yet to come for the reputation of our first president. In October 1997, the New Orleans School Board voted to rename George Washington Elementary School because its policy opposed "retaining names of schools named for former slave owners."

Washington was a man of his times and must be seen in

the context of those times. He favored the gradual abolition of slavery, and his will called for the freeing of his slaves upon the death of his wife. His views were very progressive for his day, but that fact eluded the New Orleans School Board.

Washington also does poorly in textbooks today. A recent twelve-hundred-page volume for high schools, *United States History: In the Course of Human Events,* is a model of Political Correctness, including its treatment of Washington, who is listed as one of fifteen "People Who Made a Difference." He is described as a cold man of "ordinary talents," who was more of a symbol than a genuine hero.

Washington's beloved Mount Vernon is the second most-visited home in the nation (behind the White House), "but Elvis Presley's home [in Memphis] is in third place and rising fast," according to James Rees, resident director of Mount Vernon.

Perverse Political Correctness and pervasive pop culture are not, however, the only things standing in the way of greater appreciation of George Washington and his era. Because there was no photography in the eighteenth century, our only images of Washington and his contemporaries are in engravings, drawings, and paintings. Their words come to us, not on recordings or audiotapes, but in letters and essays. Their choice of words, erratic punctuation, and random capitalization seem quaint and distant. Their powdered wigs, flowing coats, buckled shoes, and elaborate dresses give their era the quality of a fairy tale.

The Founding Fathers—Washington, Jefferson, Franklin, Adams, Hamilton, Madison, and the rest—are usually considered to have been a group of wise men working harmoniously to create that remarkable document, the Constitution of the United States of America. Wise they were, but wise because they all wanted a viable nation and they were willing to compromise to get it. Their interests varied, especially between North and South, and it was not long before these differences surfaced, eventually bringing about the Civil War.

Born in 1732 into the Virginia planter class, Washington was only twelve when his father died. Soon thereafter, he went to live with his half-brother, Lawrence, and his family at Mount Vernon. Lawrence became a role model, a substitute father, for young George.

Washington's formal education, through tutors, ended by age sixteen, when he was commissioned to survey Lord Fairfax's lands in the Shenandoah Valley. Even as a young man—one who was very tall for his day (six-feet-four in his boots)—Washington impressed people with his commanding appearance. Later known for his self-discipline, he forced himself to curb a fierce temper. Joining the Virginia militia in the French and Indian War, he learned valuable and practical lessons about warfare by observing both Indian and British Army procedures and fighting techniques. He was to make use of these lessons in the Revolutionary War.

Viewed as a hero of the French and Indian War by his fellow colonials, Washington seemed the logical choice to command the fledgling Continental Army in 1775. Underdogs against the British, the troops responded well to Washington's command. His drive and determination impressed them, and his constant efforts to get them their pay, ammunition, and supplies earned their loyalty. Not schooled in classic military strategy, Washington used audacity and surprise to foil his enemy. In 1781, at the climax of the war, he risked everything against Lord Cornwallis and the British Army at Yorktown, Virginia, and he won.

At that point, Washington did serve as a symbol—a symbol of heroism and unity—for a young country that was really a collection of sovereign states with differing backgrounds and objectives. The outpouring of admiration and love for

Washington was so universal that he almost certainly could have been crowned king of the country had he wished. He did not. On the contrary, he resigned his commission and returned to Mount Vernon until, in 1787, he was called to preside over the Constitutional Convention. There, he expressed his views only when he felt his words would have maximum influence on the outcome—which was in favor of a strong central government.

Washington dreaded political parties arising, and he hoped to maintain, through his own example, the unity that came out of the Constitutional Convention in Philadelphia. By 1790, however, Jefferson and Hamilton had split over their opinions of the French Revolution and their visions of our nation's future. Jefferson's enthusiasm for that revolution, coupled with his fundamental view of the United States as an agrarian democracy, led to the formation of the anti-Federalists (later termed Republicans, and the ancestors of the modern Democratic Party).

Hamilton, co-author of The Federalist Papers, saw the need for a strong central government to prepare our small nation for growth. He also became the rallying point for those who were appalled by the excesses of the French Revolution. The Federalists saw the specter of anarchy behind the events in France. Soon, the two sides were waging a highly partisan war of words that would be familiar to modern audiences. Bombastic speeches and newspaper articles and attacks on personal character were the ammunition in this war.

Washington tried—and ultimately failed—to bring about reconciliation between Jefferson and Hamilton. His disappointment at being unable to prevent the creation of warring political parties can be seen in his second term in frequent expressions of regret at the "extreme wretchedness of my existence while in office."

As president, Washington kept men of disparate dispositions and political views working together within his administration to get the new government organized and functioning properly. His audacity as a field commander turned to prudence as president. He weighed each issue with care before drawing a conclusion. He sensed he was the embodiment of the new republic's hopes, and he acted accordingly, with dignified restraint.

Not everyone loved Washington. John Adams, his vice president, was envious of him and considered Washington his intellectual inferior. Thomas Paine, the firebrand pamphleteer of the Revolution, who was imprisoned by his erstwhile allies during the French Revolution, turned on Washington when the latter did not immediately take up Paine's cause.

Others saw warm, gentle, and fun-loving sides of Washington. During the war years, the wife of one of his officers said that when they enjoyed picnics in the lulls between campaigns, Washington could be "impudent." A diplomat's wife commented on his graciousness as a host at Mount Vernon.

Washington put duty above personal interests, but he was always happiest at Mount Vernon, where he closely supervised the work on his seventy-six-hundred-acre farm. His gardens produced prodigious amounts of vegetables, fruits, and berries. He experimented with hybridizing. He had a threshing barn for wheat, and a grist mill. He introduced the mule to America. The fecundity of Mount Vernon was a result of his attention to detail and his enthusiasm for innovation. Even when fighting the war, and later as president, he dispatched detailed instructions to his farm managers.

In short, George Washington was not a one-dimensional mythic figure, but a complex man. As a youth he was curious, modest, resourceful, imaginative. As a patriotic commander in war, he was bold and imaginative. As a post-war leader of a new nation he was calm, reserved, prudent, magisterial, always conscious that the eyes of the nation—and the world—were on him, and that the new republic would be measured, in good part, by the world's measurement of him.

Two centuries of the world's measurement of George Washington as a man, myth, and an American patriot, are collected here.

MILESTONES IN

1732   Born February 22 in Westmoreland County, Virginia, eldest son of Augustine Washington and his second wife, Mary Ball Washington.

1743   Father dies April 12; goes to live with his half-brother, Lawrence, at Mount Vernon.

1748   Appointed to survey Lord Fairfax's lands in the Shenandoah Valley, Virginia; formal schooling ends.

1751–52   Accompanies Lawrence to Barbados, September to March (his only trip outside the country), in an effort to cure Lawrence's tuberculosis. Lawrence dies soon after their return to Mount Vernon. (George ultimately inherits the property.)

1754   Assumes command (March 20) of colonial forces sent to capture Fort Duquesne from French; defeated, surrenders to French at Fort Necessity (July 4).

1755   Appointed aide-de-camp to British General Braddock (May 10), who spurns Washington's tactical advice on the march to Fort Duquesne; Braddock killed, army routed (July 9). Washington's courage praised; appointed colonel and commander in chief of Virginia Regiment (August 14).

1758   Elected burgess for Frederick County (July 24). Leads Virginia Regiment back to Fort Duquesne, finding it abandoned by French; resigns his commission (November 23).

GEORGE WASHINGTON'S LIFE

1759   January 6, marries Martha Dandridge Custis, a wealthy Virginia widow with two children; eventually moves family to Mount Vernon.

1761   Reelected burgess (May 18).

1765   Elected to the Virginia House of Burgesses for Fairfax County (July 16; reelected 1768, '69, '71, '74).

1770   Justice of the peace, Fairfax County.

1774   Attends first Virginia Provincial Convention, Williamsburg (August); elected delegate to First Continental Congress, which meets in Philadelphia (September–October).

1775   Delegate to Second Continental Congress (May–June); elected general and commander in chief of Continental Army (June 16); takes command of troops at Cambridge, Massachusetts (July 3).

1776   His troops occupy Boston (March 16); Declaration of Independence (July 4); defeat at Battle of Long Island, and retreat to Manhattan (August 27–29); Battle of White Plains, New York (October 28); defeat of Hessians at Trenton, New Jersey (December 25–26).

1777   Defeats British at Battle of Princeton (January 3); sets up winter quarters at Morristown, New Jersey; defeated in Pennsylvania at Battle of Brandywine (September 11) and at Battle of Germantown (October 4); British general Burgoyne surrenders at Saratoga, New York (October 17); winter quarters at Valley Forge, Pennsylvania.

1778	British evacuate Philadelphia (June 18); his army outfights British force at Battle of Monmouth (June 28); makes winter quarters at Middlebrook, New Jersey.
1780	French fleet and army arrive at Newport, Rhode Island; French army under command of Comte de Rochambeau (July 11).
1781	British under Lord Cornwallis surrender at Yorktown, Virginia, to allied French and American force under Washington—including French troops under Rochambeau, and supported by a French fleet under Admiral DeGrasse (October 19).
1783	Farewell to his last-remaining officers at Fraunces Tavern, New York City (December 4); resigns commission, Annapolis, Maryland (December 23).
1787	Elected a Virginia delegate to the Constitutional Convention in Philadelphia (March 28); elected president of the convention (May 25); draft Constitution signed, convention adjourned (September 17).
1788	Elected chancellor of The College of William and Mary, Williamsburg (January 18).
1789	Elected (unanimously) President of the United States (February 4); inaugurated in Federal Hall, New York City (April 30); mother dies at Fredericksburg, Virginia (August 25); tours New England, except for Rhode Island (September–October).

1790	Visits Rhode Island (August); arrives in Philadelphia, then U.S. capital (September).
1791	Tours southern states (April–June).
1792	Elected unanimously to a second term as president (December 5).
1793	Inaugurated for second term, Independence Hall, Philadelphia (March 4); issues Proclamation of Neutrality (April 22); sets cornerstone of the President's House in the new capital city, to be called "Washington" (September 18).
1794	Declares suppression of the Whisky Rebellion (November).
1796	Farewell Address (September 17), not delivered orally, but printed in the *Daily American Advertiser* of Philadelphia.
1797	Retirement at end of second term as president; returns to Mount Vernon, upon inauguration of successor John Adams (March 4).
1798	Appointed lieutenant general and commander in chief of the Armies of the United States (July 4), with war with France a strong possibility. Does not take an active role in army.
1799	December 14, Washington dies at Mount Vernon after a bout with fever. (Martha dies at Mount Vernon on May 22, 1802.)

PART I

VOICES OF
A YOUNG
NATION

ABIGAIL ADAMS

(1744-1818)

WIFE OF PRESIDENT JOHN ADAMS,
MOTHER OF PRESIDENT JOHN QUINCY ADAMS

"...if he was not really one of the best intentioned men in the world he might be a very dangerous one."

A native of Weymouth, Massachusetts, Abigail Smith Adams was the young nation's second First Lady and was the leading figure in the social life of John Adams's presidential administration (1797-1801). Intelligent, lively, and much admired, Abigail Adams had great fondness for the Washingtons. Her extensive correspondence with her husband and with her sister, Mary Smith Cranch, records firsthand the social history of the era. The letters here are all to Mary, opening with "My dear Sister." The first two were written when John Adams was vice president; the second two when he was president. They cover a range of observations, from Washington's recovery from illness, the nature of his character, the Washingtons in a social setting, the death of Washington, and, finally, the concern Abigail shared with her husband that credit for the success of the Revolution and establishment of the new nation not be vested solely in Washington.

July 12, 1789
Richmond Hill, New York

Our august Pressident is a singular example of modesty and diffidence. He has a dignity which forbids Familiarity mixed with an easy affability which creates Love and Reverence. The fever which he had terminated in an abscess, so that he cannot sit up. Upon my second visit to Mrs. Washington he sent for me into his Chamber. He was laying upon a settee and half raising himself up, begged me to excuse his receiving me in that posture, congratulated me upon my arrival in N[ew] York and asked me how I could Relish the simple manners of America after having been accustomed to those of Europe. I replied to him that where I found simple manners I esteemed them, but that I thought we approached much nearer to the Luxury and manners of Europe according to our ability, than most persons were sensible of, and that we had our full share of taste and fondness for them. The Pressident has a Bed put into his Carriage and rides out in that way, allways with six horses and his Carriage and four attendants. Mrs. Washington accompanies him. I requested him to make Richmond Hill his resting place, and the next day he did so, but he found walking up stairs so difficult, that he has done it but once. Mrs. Washington is one of those unassuming characters which create Love & Esteem. A most becoming pleasantness sits upon her countenance & an unaffected deportment which renders her the object of veneration and Respect. With all these feelings and Sensations I found myself much more deeply impressed than I ever did before their Majesties of Britain.

January 5, 1790
Richmond Hill, New York
In the Evening [of New Year's day] I attended the drawing Room, it being Mrs. W[ashington]'s publick day. It was as much crowded as a Birth Night at St. James, and with company as Brilliantly drest, diamonds & great hoops excepted. My station is always at the right hand of Mrs. W.; through want of knowing what is right I find it sometimes occupied, but on such an occasion the President never fails of seeing that it is relinquished for me, and having removed Ladies several times, they have not learnt to rise & give it me, but this is between ourselves, as all distinction you know is unpopular. Yet this same P[resident] has so happy a faculty of appearing to accommodate & yet carrying his point, that if he was not really one of the best intentioned men in the world he might be a very dangerous one. He is polite with dignity, affable without familiarity, distant without Haughtyness, Grave without Austerity, Modest, wise and Good. These are traits in his Character which peculiarly fit him

for the exalted station he holds, and God grant
that he may Hold it with the same applause &
universal satisfaction for many years, as it is my
firm opinion that no other man could rule over
this great people & consolidate them into one
mighty Empire but he who is set over us.

Sunday Eve'ng
Decbr 22, 1799
Philadelphia

I wrote to you the day after we received the
account of the death of Gen'll Washington... No
man ever lived, more deservedly beloved and
Respected. The praise and I may say adulation
which followed his administration for several
years, never made him forget that he was a Man,
subject to the weakness and frailty attached to
human Nature. He never grew giddy, but ever
maintained a modest diffidence of his own talents, and if that was an error, it was of the
amiable and engaging kind, tho it might lead
sometimes to a want of some decisions in some
great Emergencys. Possesst of power, possesst of
an extensive influence, he never used it but for
the benefit of his Country. Witness his retirement
to private Life when Peace closed the scenes of
War; when call'd by the unanimous suffrages of
the People to the chief Majestracy of the Nation,
he acquitted himself to the satisfaction and
applause of all Good Men. When assailed by faction, when reviled by Party, he suffered with dignity, and Retired from his exalted station with a
Character which malice would not wound, nor
envy tarnish. If we look through the whole tennor

Abigail Adams

of his Life, History will not produce to us a Parrallel. Heaven has seen fit to take him from us. Our mourning is sincere, in the midst of which, we ought not to lose sight of the Blessings we have enjoy'd and still partake of, that he was spared to us, untill he saw a successor filling his place, persueing the same system which he had adopted, and that in times which have been equally dangerous and Critical. It becomes not me to say more upon this Head.

Tomorrow the Senate come in a Body with a sympathetic address, and on Thursday a Eulogy is to be delivered by Genll. Lee in the Dutch Church in this city, to which we are all invited.

Janry 28, 1800
Philadelphia
I yesterday received your Letter of the 19th. I think you have testified your proportion of Respect in a handsome manner to the Memory of the good and virtuous Washington. That he ought to live in our Memories, and be transmitted to posterity as a Character truly worth Imitation is Right, but some Eulogyst[s] have ascribed to him solely what was the joint effort & concert of Many. To no one Man in America, belongs the Epithet of Saviour of his Country. That Washington's Character, when we take into view, his Education, the place of his Birth, and the various scenes in which he was call'd to act, exhibits a most uncommon assemblage of Modesty, Moderation, Magnanimity, fortitud, perseverance and disinterestedness, will be most

readily allowed, but at no time, did the fate of America rest upon the Breath of even a Washington, and those who asset these things, are Ignorant of the spirit of their countrymen, and whilst they strive to exalt one character, degrade that of their Country. These reflections have arisen in my mind from reading Mr. [Thomas] Paynes oration and a Mad Rant of Bombast in a Boston centinal of a Mr. Messenger. Judge [George Richards] Minots oration is exempt from these reflections. Wise and judicious observations upon his Character are those only which will out live the badges of mourning. Simple Truth is his best, his greatest Eulogy. She alone can render his Fame immortal.

ABIGAIL ADAMS

JOHN ADAMS

(1735-1826)

FIRST VICE PRESIDENT, 1788-97, SECOND
PRESIDENT OF THE UNITED STATES, 1797-1801

*"...I thought him a perfectly honest Man,
with an amiable and excellent heart...."*

In later years jealous of Washington and Franklin and exceedingly vain, John Adams often complained of what he considered to be the lack of recognition due him for his role in the creation of the new nation. Unlike his firebrand cousin, Sam Adams, John, despite his later jealousy and vanity, was a man of moderate temperament. A Massachusetts native, he served on the Continental Congress's committee to draft the Declaration of Independence and argued eloquently for it. He proposed that Washington be named commander-in-chief of the Continental Army, at least in part to tie Virginia more closely to the patriot cause in the northern colonies. As a diplomat, he had a mixed record. He contributed little to the

1779 joint mission with Franklin to France to persuade the French to provide aid to the American side. Yet, when it came to the peace negotiations with England in 1783, he played an active and positive role. Back home after serving as envoy to Britain (1785-88), where the English treated him coldly, he was elected as Washington's vice president. A Federalist, he provided some balance between Jefferson and Hamilton. He was elected in 1796 to succeed Washington. The major event of his single presidential term was his decision in 1798 to keep the United States from joining the war between England and France, despite the pro-British and anti–French Revolution leanings of the Federalists. The growing anti-Federalist tide of the Jeffersonians swept the 1800 election, and Adams retired to his home in Quincy, contenting himself with writing thoughtful and respected papers on the nature of government and politics. He carried on a regular correspondence with Jefferson. By coincidence the two died on the same day, July 4, 1826. Adams and his wife, Abigail, founded a distinguished family of statesmen, diplomats, and writer. Their son, John Quincy, was elected the sixth president of the United States in 1824.

On the 5th of August [1774] Congress assembled in Carpenters Hall. The Day before, I dined with Mr. Lynch, a delegate from South Carolina who...after some Observations had been made on the Eloquence of Mr. Patrick Henry and Mr. Richard Henry Lee, which had been very loudly celebrated by the Virginians, said that the most eloquent Speech that had ever been made in Virginia or anywhere else, upon American Affairs had been made by Colonel

JOHN ADAMS

Washington. This was the first time I had ever heard the Name of Washington, as a Patriot in our present Controversy, I asked who is Colonel Washington and what was his Speech? Colonel Washington he said was the officer who had been famous in the late French War and in the Battle in which Braddock fell. His Speech was that if the Bostonians should be involved in Hostilities with the British Army he would march to their relief at the head of a Thousand Men at his own expence. This Sentence, Mr. Lynch said, had more Oratory in it, in his Judgment, than all that he had ever heard or read. We all agreed that it was both sublime, pathetic and beautifull.

—From the *Autobiography of John Adams*

[I]…have observed at home, and abroad, that Eloquence in public Assemblies is not the surest road, to Fame and Preferment, at least unless it is used with great caution, very rarely, and with great Reserve. The examples of Washington, Franklin and Jefferson are enough to shew that Silence and reserve in public are more Efficacious than Argumentation or Oratory.

—Ibid.

General Knox came up to dine with me at Braintree. The design of his Visit was as I soon perceived to sound me in relation to General Washington. He asked me what my Opinion of him was. I answered with the Utmost Frankness, that I thought him a perfectly honest Man, with

an amiable and excellent heart, and the most
important Character at that time among Us, for
he was the Center of our Union. He asked the
question, he said, because, as I was going to
Europe it was of importance that the Generals
Character should be supported in other
Countries. I replied that he might be perfectly at
ease on the Subject for he might depend upon it,
that both from principle and Affection, public
and private I should do my Utmost to support
his Character at all times and in all places, unless
something should happen very greatly to alter my
Opinion of him, and this I have done from that
time to this. I mention this incident, because that
insolent Blasphemer of things sacred and tran-
scendent Libeller of all that is good, Tom Paine,
has more than once asserted in Print, the scandalous Lye, that I was one of a Faction in the fall
of the Year 1777, against General Washington.

—Ibid. Referring to a meeting
on the eve of Adams's first mission to France

I have been distressed to see some members of
this house disposed to idolize an image which
their own hands have molten. I speak here of the
superstitious veneration that is sometimes paid to
General Washington. Altho' I honour him for his
good qualities, yet in this house I feel myself his
Superior.

—Comment made in the Continental Congress, 1777

JOHN ADAMS

Would Washington ever have been Commander of the Revolutionary Army or President of the United States if he had not married the rich widow of Mr. Custis?

—Quoted in Thomas Hutchinson's *History of the Colony and Province of Massachusetts Bay* (1936)

That Washington was not a scholar is certain. That he was too illiterate, unlearned and unread for his station and reputation is equally past dispute.

—Quoted by Marcus Cunliffe in *George Washington, Man and Monument* (1958)

THE AURORA

c. 1790s NEWSPAPER

"...the American nation has been deceived by Washington."

At the distance of two centuries we tend to think of the Founding Fathers as a group of serious gentlemen working in harmony. To an extent they did, but human nature was still human nature. There were personality clashes, suspicions about motives, and sharp differences over basic policy. One of Washington's greatest accomplishments was to keep such disparate men as Hamilton and Jefferson together in his cabinet. Although Washington wished there to be no political parties, their development proved to be unavoidable. Jefferson was deeply influenced by the high-minded early leaders of the French Revolution. With friction growing between France and England, and war on the horizon (it broke out in 1793), he and his supporters formed the Republican Party and leaned toward France. Hamilton and his supporters were appalled by the turn toward violence in

France and formed the Federalists—using a term originally applied to all supporters of the new Constitution when it was being drafted and ratified. They leaned toward England. The Jeffersonians suspected Federalists of secretly planning to abandon the republican form of government for a monarchy. (Jefferson called them "Monocrats"—for "monarchists and aristocrats.") Washington maintained neutrality in this issue, although in the final months of his presidency, many felt he was leaning to an anti-French position. By the time his vice president, John Adams, a Federalist, was elected to succeed him in 1797, passions were running high between the two party groups.

The *Aurora* was an anti-Federalist newspaper published by Benjamin Franklin Bache, a grandson of Benjamin Franklin. It launched scathing attacks on President Washington, two of which follow. The *National Gazette,* published by Philip Freneau—dubbed "the Poet of the Revolution," and employed as a translating clerk in Jefferson's Secretary of State office—propagandized for the Republican cause and also attacked Washington. The Federalist-Republican clashes strained Washington's relationship with Jefferson, although it did not break. With Jefferson as their candidate, the Republicans won the election of 1800 (ultimately becoming the Democratic Party). By 1820, the Federalists had disappeared as a party.

If ever a nation has been debauched by a man, the American nation has been debauched by Washington. If ever a nation has been deceived by a man, the American nation has been deceived by Washington. Let his conduct, then, be an example for future ages. Let it serve to be a warning that no man may be an idol. Let the history of the

Federal government instruct mankind that the mask of patriotism may be worn to conceal the foulest designs against the liberties of a people.

—From an edition early in 1797

When a retrospect is taken of the Washingtonian administration of eight years, it is the subject of the greatest astonishment that a single individual should have cankered the principles of Republicanism in an enlightened people, just emerged from the gulf of despotism, and should have carried his designs against the public liberty so far as to put in jeopardy its very existence. Such, however, are the facts, and with them staring us in the face, this day ought to be a jubilee in the United States.

—From the edition of March 4, 1797, the inauguration day of John Adams as President Washington's successor

MARTHA DANGERFIELD BLAND

WIFE OF A VIRGINIA COLONEL, FRIEND OF THE WASHINGTONS

"He can be downright impudent sometimes...."

Martha Dangerfield Bland was the wife of Theodorick Bland, a Virginia colonel of dragoons. In March 1777, Martha Washington went from Mount Vernon to Morristown, New Jersey, to look after General Washington at his headquarters, following a severe illness (probably the flu) that he had endured for ten days. With the arrival of Mrs. Washington, a number of officers' wives, including Mrs. Bland, flocked to the headquarters. She and her husband were frequent visitors as spring blossomed. She captured a lighter side of George Washington in a letter to her sister.

Now let me speak of our noble and agreeable commander, for he commands both sexes, one by his excellent skill in military matters, the other by his ability, politeness and attention.... From dinner till night he is free for all company. His worthy lady seems to be in perfect felicity when she is by the side of her "Old Man" as she calls him. We often make parties on horseback. General Washington throws off the hero and takes on the chatty, agreeable companion. He can be downright impudent sometimes—such impudence, Fanny, as you and I like.

—Letter, March 1777

MARTHA DANGERFIELD BLAND

NAPOLEON BONAPARTE
(1769-1821)

FRENCH SOLDIER, EMPEROR, EXILE

"They wanted me to be another Washington."

In 1792, the French monarchy was overthrown in the revolution, and young Napoleon—unlike most army officers—sided with the revolutionaries. He rose in power as his tactical brilliance took him to victory after victory and, in 1799, joined a plot to overthrow the French Directory, replacing it with the Consulate. Within three years he was made First Consul for life, soon crowning himself Emperor Napoleon I. In 1803, war broke out with England, Russia, Austria, and Sweden; by 1805, Napoleon's armies had crushed all rivals but England, which was protected by the sea and her powerful navy. During the first decade of the century, France dominated much of continental Europe. Napoleon installed various relatives as heads of states he controlled. His audacious invasion of Russia in 1812 proved a disaster, and he was forced to retreat, with several hundred thousand troops dying from freezing temperatures and starvation on the way. The allies—England, Austria, Prussia, and Russia—joined forces and, in 1814, captured Paris, forcing Napoleon to abdicate. He was exiled to Elba, off the west coast of Italy. In 1815, he escaped to France and for a time—called The Hundred Days—he returned to his past glory, which ended that spring with defeat in the Battle of Waterloo. Exiled to the remote South Atlantic island of St. Helena, Napoleon often ruminated on his lost empire. Bold, daring, and resourceful, Napoleon Bonaparte lacked Washington's patience, reflective qualities, and consensus-building ability.

They wanted me to be another Washington.

—The above quotation is from a letter by Benjamin West, the painter, to Rufus King, May 3, 1797, published in *Literary History of the United States* (1963). This was soon after Napoleon's early victories, when he had begun to see himself as the potential leader of a great French empire.

EDWARD BRADDOCK

(1695-1755)

BRITISH GENERAL

"These are high times...."

Although he had been in the Coldstream Guards since 1710, Edward Braddock had seen little action before being posted to Virginia in February 1755, with the rank of major general and commander-in-chief of British forces in North America. Braddock's main objective was Fort Duquesne (site of Pittsburgh), a key French stronghold. He had fourteen hundred regular troops and seven hundred colonial militiamen, although he considered the latter of little value. Anxious to take Fort Duquesne before it could be reinforced, Braddock on June 10 led some twelve hundred men from Cumberland, Maryland, with the wagon supply train and the remainder of the soldiers to follow. On the morning of July 9, the troops forded the Monongahela River and advanced in a column—European style—toward the enemy post.

Washington, a twenty-three-year-old Virginia militia officer familiar with Indian tactics, ventured to advise General Braddock to disperse his troops in open order so they would not be vulnerable to ambush in the deep forest. The haughty Braddock's dismissive reply has been recorded for history. Soon thereafter, the massed troops were subjected to a sudden volley of gunfire, along with a rain of arrows and terrifying war whoops, from a force of some nine hundred French, Indians, and Canadians. The British fought bravely, but were routed, with nearly a thousand casualties, including Braddock, who was mortally wounded. Washington rallied the remaining troops, who retreated from the battlefield, taking their dying general with them.

These are high times when a British general is to take counsel of a Virginia buckskin.

—Remark, while on the march to Fort Duquesne, July 1755, rejecting Washington's advice to open up marching column formations to avoid a French and Indian ambush.

EDWARD BRADDOCK

CHARLES JAMES FOX

(1749-1806)

ENGLISH STATESMAN AND ORATOR

*"For him it has been reserved to run the race of glory,
without experiencing the smallest interruption
to the brilliancy of his career."*

Whether in or out of government, Charles James Fox was a frequent thorn in the side of George III's prime ministers. He entered Parliament in 1768 and within two years headed the Admiralty under Lord North's government. Disagreements with North led to his dismissal in 1774. Embittered, he joined the opposition and used his brilliant oratorical skills to denounce the government's American war policy. Disliked by the king, he nevertheless became foreign secretary in the Whig government of Rockingham in 1782. When Lord Shelburne succeeded Rockingham, Fox was dismissed. Then still a Whig leader, he aligned himself with the Tory opposition to defeat Shelburne's government. As a result, he again became foreign secretary for a brief time. After 1789, he became firmly committed to opposition of William Pitt's government by favoring the French Revolution and demanding non-intervention by England. On Pitt's death in 1806, Fox became foreign secretary for the third and final time. Shortly before his death, Fox proposed legislation to abolish the slave trade. It was passed the next year.

I cannot, indeed, help admiring the wisdom and fortune of this great man. By the phrase "fortune," I mean not in the smallest degree to derogate from his merit. But, notwithstanding his extraordinary talents and exalted integrity, it must be considered as singularly fortunate, that he should have experienced a lot, which so seldom falls to the portion of humanity, and have passed through such a variety of scenes, without stain and without reproach. It must, indeed, create astonishment, that placed in circumstances so critical, and filling for a series of years a station so conspicuous, his character should never once have been called in question; that he should in no one instance have been accused either of improper insolence, or of mean submission, in his transactions with foreign nations. For him it has been reserved, to run the race of glory, without experiencing the smallest interruption to the brilliancy of his career.

—January 31, 1794

CHARLES JAMES FOX

BENJAMIN FRANKLIN
(1706-90)

STATESMAN, WRITER, PRINTER, SCIENTIST

*"You would, at this side of the sea,
enjoy the great reputation you have acquired."*

Learned, charming, urbane, and witty, Franklin came from humble beginnings. The son of a Boston candle and soap maker, he left school at age ten to help his father. He soon moved to his half-brother's printing shop as an apprentice and occasional ghostwriter for the brother's periodical. In 1723 he moved to Philadelphia and by 1730 was owner of the *Pennsylvania Gazette*. His common sense philosophy and lively writing gained the newspaper great popularity. His *Poor Richard's Almanack* (1732-57) contained many aphorisms that have become standard American proverbs to this day. His autobiography, covering only his youthful years, is still considered one of the best of that genre. He helped establish an academy that ultimately became the University of

Pennsylvania. His interest in science led to his invention of a number of things, including bifocals and the glass harmonica. He conducted a spectacular experiment during a thunderstorm, flying a kite to prove the connection between lightning and electricity. Despite his great liking for England—living there for a time—as troubles with the colonies deepened, he threw himself into the American cause, serving as a delegate to the first Continental Congress and as a member of the committee that drafted the Declaration of Independence in 1776. Late that year, he sailed for France as a diplomatic minister to that American ally. There he was popular and effective. In 1780, he wrote the letter quoted below to Washington, for whom he had great affection and high regard. He deplored the sniping that critics directed at Washington's conduct of the war. Franklin went on to serve as one of the negotiators of what became the Treaty of Paris of 1783, concluding the war. He returned to America in 1785 as president of the Pennsylvania council. His last great contribution to his country was his participation in the Constitutional Convention of 1787 and his efforts to have it ratified. In the last year of his life, he added a codicil to his will, leaving one of his most prized possessions to Washington as a mark of his esteem.

Should peace arrive after another campaign or two, and afford us a little leisure, I should be happy to see your Excellency in Europe and to accompany you, if my age and strength would permit, in visiting some of its ancient and most famous kingdoms. You would, at this side of the sea, enjoy the great reputation you have acquired, pure and free from those little shades that the jealousy and envy of a man's countrymen and contemporaries are ever endeavouring

BENJAMIN FRANKLIN

to cast over living merit. Here you would know, and enjoy, what posterity will say of Washington. For a thousand leagues have nearly the same effect with a thousand years. The feeble voice of those grovelling passions cannot extend so far either in time or distance. At present I enjoy that pleasure for you, as I frequently hear the old generals of this martial country (who study the maps of America and mark upon them all your operations) speak with sincere approbation and great applause of your conduct; and join in giving you the character of one of the greatest captains of the age.

—Letter to George Washington from Paris, March 5, 1780

My fine crab-tree walking-stick, with a gold head curiously wrought in the form of a cap of liberty, I give to my friend, and the friend of mankind, General Washington. If it were a sceptre, he has merited it and would become it.

—Codicil added by Franklin to his will, June 23, 1789

PHILIP FRENEAU

(1752-1832)

POET, PROPAGANDIST

"Even Cincinnatus received no adulation of this kind...."

A Princeton classmate of James Madison, Freneau was both soldier and privateer during the Revolutionary War. He was captured by the British and imprisoned aboard the ship *Aurora*. It was there in 1780 that he wrote the poem "The British Prison Ship." His spirited verses earned him the nickname "Poet of the Revolution." He later twice returned to sea as a captain (1785–89 and 1802–04). His hyperbolic praise of Washington was, at first, unmatched. In 1791, Jefferson's Republicans launched a newspaper in Philadelphia, the *National Gazette,* and Freneau became editor of this important propaganda outlet. In it he relentlessly attacked the Federalists, especially Vice President John Adams. By 1792, however, he had trained his fire on Washington. The president's sin: his reserved manner, which Freneau interpreted as a fondness for pomp and thus monarchism!

He comes!—the Genius of these lands—
 Fame's thousand tongues his worth confess,
Who conquered with his suffering bands,
 And grew immortal in distress.

—Poem on the occasion of General Washington's
arrival at Philadelphia, 1775

Even Cincinnatus received no adulation of this
kind.... Surely the office itself [the presidency] is
a sufficient testimony of the people's favor, without worshipping him likewise.

—Comment in the *National Gazette,* February 27, 1793,
protesting public celebration of Washington's birthday

GEORGE III

(1738-1820)

KING OF GREAT BRITAIN AND IRELAND, 1760-1820

"...the most distinguished of any man living."

Greatly influenced by his mother ("George, be a king!"), George III determined, on his accession to the throne, to rule as well as to reign. He went through a succession of prime ministers until he found one, Lord North (1770-82), who saw eye to eye with him. Already, the Sugar Act (1764) and Stamp Act (1765) were causing trouble to brew in America. North's policies of coercion became the last straw. Meanwhile, Canada and India had been secured for England during the 1760s. William Pitt (the Younger) succeeded North at the end of the Revolution in 1783, and his Tories won a sweeping election victory the next year, establishing the custom of "going to the country" for a mandate. As a result, Parliament was able to curb George III's stubborn, but conscientious, impulses. George had a gentle side, was devoted to his wife, Charlotte, and was fond of farming. During his long reign, the Industrial Revolution burst forth, and the arts flourished. From 1780 on, he suffered bouts of what were believed to be insanity but now are considered to have been a nervous disorder, and in 1810 was supplanted by his son, the Prince of Wales, as regent (who later ruled as the dissolute, mean-spirited George IV).

[This] placed him in a light the most distinguished of any man living....
The greatest character of the age.

—Attributed to George III, commenting on Washington's retirement from the presidency in 1797 and his 1783 resignation as commander in chief.

ALEXANDER HAMILTON
(1757-1804)

AIDE-DE-CAMP TO GENERAL WASHINGTON, SECRETARY OF THE TREASURY TO PRESIDENT WASHINGTON

"I trust...that you will determine to make a further sacrifice of your tranquillity and happiness to the public good."

Hamilton, who was the first of the major Founding Fathers to die, was handsome, a persuasive orator, egotistical and aristocratic by inclination. Born out of wedlock on the Caribbean island of Nevis, he had an opportunity when the businessman to whom he had been apprenticed sent him to King's College (now Columbia) in 1774. There he began to write articles in favor of the patriot cause (they were often attributed to John Jay) and, when war broke out, he joined as a captain of artillery. Coming to Washington's attention, he soon was the general's aide-de-camp. In 1781, he performed brilliantly in the field in the battle of Yorktown. He married

Elizabeth Schuyler, daughter of one of New York's wealthiest men. He became a lawyer and a member of the Continental Congress. As early as 1780 he drafted a plan for a government with more federal power than existed under the Articles of Confederation. A delegate to the Constitutional Convention, he did much to get the new Constitution ratified, especially with his contributions to The Federalist Papers.

As Washington's first secretary of the treasury, he set out to put the nation's finances on a sound footing. He proposed to pay in full the federal government's domestic debt, and to have the government assume state debts, raise excise taxes, and enact protective tariffs. Despite Washington's desire to avoid the creation of political parties, Hamilton and Adams, with their desire for stronger central government (and intimations of an industrial future) soon headed the Federalists, and Jefferson led the anti-Federalists, who agreed with his vision of a decentralized agrarian democracy. Hamilton did not get his tariffs, but the assumption of state debt was achieved when he traded support for a Southern capital with Jefferson in exchange for the latter's support.

Hamilton foresaw the day when the nation would be an economic superpower, growing rich on commerce, with states being subsidiary to the federal government and slavery only a memory. His influence waned after 1795, when he resigned from the cabinet. He did assist Washington with his Farewell Address to the Nation. He suffered personal tragedies with the loss of his eldest son in a duel in 1801. His daughter went mad with shock as a result. In the presidential election of 1800, tied between Jefferson and Aaron Burr, he had the Federalists in the House of Representatives throw their support to the former. Despite this, Hamilton, impatient and blunt, lacked the political skills of a Jefferson or a Madison, and had no power after the Republicans (anti-Federalists) came to power. Meanwhile, Burr nurtured a bitter grudge against him for his actions in the 1800 election. This deepened four years later, when Hamilton thwarted Burr's ambitions to become governor of New York. Burr claimed Hamilton had called him publicly a "dangerous man" (probably true). Hamilton's reply was evasive, so Burr challenged him to a duel. It took place in Weehawken, New Jersey, across the Hudson River from New York City. Hamilton, who withheld direct fire, was mortally wounded. He was forty-seven.

It was not long before I discovered that he [Washington] was neither remarkable for delicacy or good temper.

—Letter to Philip Schuyler, Hamilton's father-in-law,
February 18, 1781

30 July 1792
Philadelphia
I received the most sincere pleasure at finding in our last conversation, that there was some relaxation in the disposition you had before discovered to decline a re election. Since your departure, I have lost no opportunity of sounding the opinions of persons, whose opinions were worth knowing, on these two points. 1st the effect of your declining upon the public affairs, and upon your own reputation, 2dly the effect of your continuing, in reference to the declarations you have made of your disinclination to public

ALEXANDER HAMILTON

life—And I can truly say, that I have not found the least difference of sentiment, on either point. The impression is uniform—that your declining would be to be deplored as the greatest evil, that could befall the country at the present juncture, and as critically hazardous to your own reputation—that your continuance will be justified in the mind of every friend to his country by the evident necessity for it. Tis clear, says every one, with whom I have conversed, that the affairs of the national government are not yet firmly established—that its enemies, generally speaking, are as inveterate as ever—that their enmity has been sharpened by its success and by all the resentments which flow from disappointed predictions and mortified vanity—that a general and strenuous effort is making in every state to place the administration of it in the hand of its enemies, as if they were its safest guardians—that the period of the next house of representatives is likely to prove the crisis of its permanent character—that if you continue in office nothing materially mischievous is to be apprehended—if you quit much is to be dreaded—the same motives which induced you to accept originally ought to decide you to continue till matters have assumed a more determinate aspect—that indeed it would have been better, as it regards your own character, that it had never consented to come forward, than now to leave the business unfinished and in danger of being undone—that in the event of storms arising there would be imputation either of want of foresight or want of firmness—and, in fine, that on public and personal accounts, on patriotic and prudential considerations, the clear path to be pursued by you will be again to obey the voice of your country; which it is noted doubted will be as earnest and unanimous as ever....

I trust, Sir, and I pray God that you will determine to make a further sacrifice to your tranquillity and happiness to the public good. I trust that it need not continue above a year or two more—And I think that it will be more eligible to retire from office before the expiration of the term of an election, than to decline a re election.

The sentiments I have delivered upon this occasion, I can truly say, proceed exclusively from an anxious concern for the public welfare and an affectionate personal attachment.

—Letter to George Washington, imploring him to stand for election to a second term as president

If virtue can secure happiness in another world, he is happy.

—Letter to W. B. Giles, January 2, 1800, following Washington's death

ALEXANDER HAMILTON

SIR WILLIAM HOWE
(1729-1814)

BRITISH GENERAL

"I...forewarn you of the Calamities which may ensue...."

William Howe, the younger brother of Admiral Richard Howe, distinguished himself in the French and Indian War in the fight for Quebec (1760). In 1775 he arrived at Boston with reinforcements for General Thomas Gage and commanded the British troops in the battle of Bunker Hill. Later that year he succeeded Gage as commander in chief, thus becoming Washington's counterpart. The next year he withdrew his troops from besieged Boston to Halifax, Nova Scotia. He then led his forces against Washington's in the successful Battle of Long Island, which led to British control of most of southeast New York and much of New Jersey. In 1777 he led a successful drive on Philadelphia, defeating Washington at the Battle of Brandywine. He was able to hold Philadelphia by beating off an American attack at

Germantown, Pennsylvania, but was unable to wipe out the Continental Army. Bitter at what he considered insufficient support from his government, he resigned in 1778 and returned to England. Howe's letter to Washington, complaining of the latter's army's perfectly normal wartime behavior, drew a sardonic reply.

Sir,

Your Parties having destroyed several Mills in the adjacent Country, which can only distress the peaceable Inhabitants residing in their Houses, I am constrained from a Regard to their Sufferings, and a sense of the Duty I owe to the Public, to forewarn you of the Calamities which may ensue, and to express my Abhorrence of such Proceedings. At the same Time I am inclined to believe that the Outrages already committed have not been in consequence of your Orders, and that this early Notice will engage you to put an effectual Stop to them; If not, I do in the most direct Terms disclaim any share in creating the general Scene of Distress among the Inhabitants, which such Destruction must Inevitably cause. With due respect, I am, &c.

W. Howe

—Letter to General Washington
from headquarters, October 3, 1777

(Washington's reply)
Head Quarters, October 6, 1777
I am happy to find you express so much sensibility to the suffering of the Inhabitants, as it gives room to hope, that those wanton and unneces-

SIR WILLIAM HOWE

sary depredations, which have heretofore in too
many instances, marked the conduct of your
Army, will be discontinued for the future. The
instances I allude to need not be enumerated,
your own Memory will suggest them to your
imagination, from the destruction of Charles
Town in Massachusetts, down to the More
recent burning of Mills, Barnes and Houses at
the Head of Elk, and in the vicinity of the
Schuylkill. I am etc.

A second message the same day—written by Hamilton on
behalf of Washington—serves as an amusing postscript:

General Washington's compliments to General
Howe. He does himself the pleasure to return
him a dog, which accidentally fell into his hands,
and by the inscription on the Collar, appears to
belong to General Howe.

THOMAS JEFFERSON

(1743-1826)

WASHINGTON'S SECRETARY OF STATE,
THIRD PRESIDENT OF THE UNITED STATES, 1801-09

*"He was...in every sense of the words,
a wise, a good, and a great man."*

Eleven years younger than Washington, Jefferson, like Washington, was born to the Virginia planter class. He acquired his devotion to democracy at an early age. He studied law at The College of William and Mary; then served in the Virginia House of Burgesses (1769-75), where he was a leader of the patriot faction. Brilliant in written argumentation, he was not an effective public speaker. In 1775 he was (except for minor adjustments made by Benjamin Franklin and Adams) the author of the Declaration of Independence. Back in Virginia, in the new state legislature, his proposals to abolish primogeniture (to prevent continuation of aristocracy) and establish laws of religious freedom were passed.

Those to establish public schools, a university and, a library system did not pass. In 1779 he succeeded Patrick Henry as governor of Virginia. He served during the later years of the American Revolution, when Virginia was invaded by the British.

Following the war, he was in the Continental Congress (1783-84) where he devised the decimal system of coinage, based upon the dollar, and proposed an ordinance for governing the Northwest Territory. In 1785, he succeeded Franklin as minister to France and was there at the beginning of the French Revolution in 1789, to which he was sympathetic. On the other hand, his unsuccessful joint effort with John Adams to negotiate a trade treaty with England left him with a strongly negative view of that country. Although he was overseas when the Constitution was adopted, he expressed his support for a stronger central government and the Bill of Rights. He returned to America in 1790 to be Washington's secretary of state. Considering himself neither a Federalist nor an anti-Federalist, he concentrated at first on working for unity within the young government.

His differences with Alexander Hamilton began to surface over the best way to persuade England to give up the Northwest forts, which it had not done, in violation of the Treaty of Paris of 1783. They clashed over Hamilton's Bank of the United States scheme. Jefferson became alarmed at what he saw as Hamilton's and the Federalists' monarchist tendencies, and assumed leadership of the anti-Federalist political forces. The members of his circle began to call themselves "Republicans" (today's Democratic Party traces its roots to this). In 1791, they established the *National Gazette,* edited by Philip Freneau, as the party's house organ. For a time, President Washington was successful in keeping both

Jefferson and Hamilton working in his cabinet, but in 1793 Jefferson resigned. In 1796, running for president, he placed second and, in keeping with the method of the time, became vice president to Adams. While Adams's Federalists were split with dissension, Jefferson led the Republicans to growth. In the presidential election of 1800, Jefferson and Aaron Burr were tied, throwing the decision to the House of Representatives. Ironically, Hamilton persuaded the Federalists in the House to support Jefferson because he considered Jefferson to be less dangerous than Burr.

Jefferson's greatest achievements as president were the Louisiana Purchase (1803), increasing the nation's size by one hundred and forty percent and from which all or part of thirteen more states were carved, and the Lewis and Clark expedition (1803-06) to find a practicable land route to the Pacific Coast. The expedition had an incalculable effect on the development of the American West. In 1809, Jefferson retired to Monticello, his Virginia estate. He remained an influential intellectual, philosopher, scientist, and architect. He had the satisfaction of seeing his University of Virginia become a reality at Charlottesville. And, his successors as president, disciples James Madison and James Monroe, consulted him frequently. Over the years, Jefferson expressed a sophisticated appreciation of George Washington's essentiality to the creation of the new nation.

His memory will be adored while liberty shall have votaries, his name will triumph over time and will in future ages assume its just station among the most celebrated worthies of the world.

—From *Notes on the State of Virginia,* 1784

THOMAS JEFFERSON

[Washington] errs as other men do, but errs with integrity.

—From a letter to William B. Giles, December 31, 1795

His mind was great and powerful, without being of the very first order; his penetration strong, though not as acute as that of a Newton, Bacon, or Locke; and as far as he saw, no judgment was ever sounder. It was slow in operation, being little aided by invention or imagination, but sure in conclusion.... He was incapable of fear, meeting personal dangers with the calmest unconcern. His integrity was most pure, his justice the most inflexible I have ever known.... He was, indeed, in every sense of the words, a wise, a good, and a great man.

—From a letter to Dr. Walter Jones, January 2, 1814

Few men lived whose opinions were more unbiased and correct. Not that it is pretended he never felt bias. His passions were naturally strong, but his reason, generally stronger.... He possessed the love, veneration and confidence of all.

—The Anas, February 4, 1818

MARQUIS DE LAFAYETTE
(1757-1834)

FRENCH GENERAL, PATRIOT, AND STATESMAN

*"Give me leave, My dear General,
to present you with a picture of the Bastille...."*

Born to an aristocratic family, the young army officer Marie Joseph Paul Yves Roch Gilbert du Motier marquis de Lafayette was charged with enthusiasm for the American Revolution. Despite obstacles from the officially neutral French government, he left France at age twenty for Philadelphia to join Washington's army. The Continental Congress quickly appointed him a major general. He plunged into the war, soon became a close friend of Washington's (for whom he always showed the greatest respect), was wounded at the Battle of Brandywine, shared the privations of Valley Forge during the winter of 1777, and was given a divisional command. He returned to France (1779-80) and negotiated for French aid to the American cause. Returning once again to America, he distinguished himself in the climactic battle of the war at Yorktown in 1781. In the early stages of the revolution in France—where he was immensely popular—he was elected vice president of the National Assembly, and the day after the Bastille fell in 1789 he became commander of the National Guard. He designed the French tricolor flag that year. He sought to be moderating influence between contending factions. Briefly, in 1792, he even tried to save the monarchy. The same year, he failed to turn his army on republican forces as extremists took over Paris. He fled the country, was captured and imprisoned in Austria from 1792-97. Liberated by Napoleon, he lived in retirement, returning to America 1824-25 to an enthusiastic welcome. His integrity, bravery and idealism made him an ideal symbol of ties between the United States and France.

> *Paris,*
> *March the 17th, 1790*
> *My dear General [Washington]*
> Our Revolution is Getting on as Well as it Can With a Nation that Has Swalled [swallowed] up liberty all at once, and is still liable to Mistake licentiousness for freedom—the Assembly Have More Hatred to the Ancient System than Experience on the proper Organization of a New and Constitutional Government—the Ministers are lamenting the loss of power, and Affraid to use that which they Have—and As Every thing has been destroied and Not much New Building is Yet Above Ground, there is Much Room for Critics and Calomnies.

To this May be Added that We still are Pestered
By two parties, the Aristocratic that is panting
for a Counter Revolution, and the fractious
Which Aims at the division of the Empire, and
destruction of all Authority and perhaps the lifes
of the Reigning Branch, Both of which parties
are fomenting trouble.

Give me leave, My dear General, to present you
With a picture of the Bastille just as it looked a
few days after I Had ordered its demolition, with
the Main Kea [key] of that fortress of despotism—it is a tribute Which I owe as A Son to
My Adoptived father, as an aid de Camp to
My General, as a Missionary of liberty to its
patriarch.

Adieu, My Beloved General. My Most
Affectionate Respects Wait on Mrs. Washington,
present me most affectionately to George, to
Hamilton, Knox, Harrison, Jay, Humphrey and
all friends. Most tenderly and respectfully Your
Most Affectionate and filial friend.

Lafayette

HENRY "LIGHT-HORSE HARRY" LEE

(1756-1818)

REVOLUTIONARY WAR HERO, GOVERNOR OF VIRGINIA

"...first in war..."

From a leading Virginia family, Henry Lee joined the Continental Army in 1777 and soon came to Washington's attention. He distinguished himself with "great skill and bravery" in numerous battles, according to nineteenth-century historian Benson Lossing. As a cavalry commander, his service under General Nathaniel Greene in the Carolina campaigns from 1780 onward was particularly daring and brilliant. In 1785 he was elected to the Continental Congress and was active in the effort to ratify the new Constitution. In 1792 he was elected governor of Virginia, and in 1799 returned to

Congress. On December 19, the day after receiving the news that Washington had died on the 14th, a Congressional committee set December 26 as a day of mourning in Philadelphia, then the capital city. Resolutions drafted by Lee and James Madison were presented to Congress by John Marshall. The day of mourning began with the firing of sixteen cannons, repeated every half hour until 11 a.m. Lee delivered the eulogy from the pulpit of the city's Lutheran Church.

While Lee's wartime service was distinguished and his patriotism unblemished, he was a poor business manager (at one point imprisoned for debts), and in 1817 he left his wife and children (among them the future Confederate General Robert E. Lee) for the West Indies and died the following year.

First in war, first in peace, and first in the hearts of his countrymen, he was second to none in the humble and endearing scenes of private life. Pious, just, humane, temperate and sincere—uniform, dignified and commanding—his example was as edifying to all around him as were the effects of that example lasting.... Such was the man for whom the nation mourns.

—From an oration at a public memorial service for Washington, Philadelphia, December 26, 1799

Henry Lee

HENRIETTA LISTON
WIFE OF THE BRITISH MINISTER TO
THE UNITED STATES, 1796-1800

*"He possesses so much natural unaffected dignity, and is so
noble a figure as to always give a pleasing impression."*

Henrietta Liston was a newlywed when she and her husband, Robert, left for Philadelphia. He was to replace George Hammond whose relations with American officialdom had been rocky. Since the signing of the Jay Treaty, Anglo-American relations had been improving. Henrietta was much younger than her husband, then in his fifties (he had entered diplomatic service when he was nearly forty). In the young nation's capital, Robert Liston contributed materially to the American-British rapprochement at a time when the U.S. and France nearly went to war with one another.

The Listons were well liked; U.S. Republicans, however, favoring France, frequently launched verbal assaults at Liston as the representative of their arch-enemy, England. During

their years in the United States, Mrs. Liston wrote frequently
to her uncle in Glasgow, Scotland; the following are excerpts
from those letters.

German Town [Pennsylvania]
6 Sept 1796

We reached Mount Vernon next day to dinner, and were received with the utmost
kindness by the President and Mrs. Washington,
his Family consists of the Marquis la Fayettes
Son, and his Tutor, the former a gentle, melan-
choly, interesting youth, the latter clever and
accomplished but apparently proud and sullen.—
the President's Secretary, a modest young Man,
and a Miss Custis, the Grand Daughter of Mrs
Washington by a former Marriage, one of the
prettiest Girls I have seen.— As Mr. Liston was
anxious to reach home by the arrival of the packet, and desirous of extending his journey to the
Vale of Winchester, We departed after three days
stay, in spight of entreaties:—the President was at
great pains to show Us every part of his Farm, He
is, indeed, one of the best Farmers in America,
and it seems to be his favourite occupation....

Philadelphia
Monday 31st October 1796

Mr. Liston and I were yesterday in Town at a
publick Dinner of the Presidents. I was as usual
on his right hand and we had a great deal of conversation—as the conduct of the French Minister
during this Election has very much disgusted
Washington and his Ministers he seemed to show
even more than usual attention to Mr. Liston and

HENRIETTA LISTON

Me. The spirits of the Party I imagine were a little damped in the evening when when the Proclamation came that Jeffersons ticket had gained the Election in this state—it is still possible that Adams may ultimately succeed, and even possible that Pinckney, late Minister in London may become President—this arises from the peculiar Mode of voting for President and Vice President at the same time without particularizing which is the former and which the latter, so that in March when the matter is decided the Majority of votes carry it and this Majority may render the Man President who the People intended as vice President yet present appearances are in favor of Jefferson chiefly from the indefatigable pains and unjustifiable means used by his party—

Philadelphia
9th Dec. 1796

Yesterday tempted me abroad to hear the Presidents speech, at the opening of Congress, the last He may, probably, ever make in publick.—the Hall was crowded and a prodigious Mob at the Door, about twelve oClock Washington entered in full dress, as He always is on publick occasions.... He was preceded by the Sergeant at Arms, with his Mace—He bowed on each side as He past to an arm chair upon a platform raised some steps from the ground and railed-in; after composing himself He drew a paper from his pocket.—Washington writes better than he reads, there is even a little hesitation in his common speaking, but He possesses so much natural unaffected dignity, and is so noble a figure as to give always a pleasing impression. I happened to sit very near him, and as every Person stood-up at his entrance and again when He began to read I had an opportunity of seeing the extreme agitation He felt when He mentioned the French. He is, I believe, very much inraged, this is the second French Minister who has insulted him....

Norfolk
8 Dec. 1797
I mentioned by the past Packet Mr. Liston's intention and mine to accompany my Brother and his Party to Norfolk, taking them to Mount Vernon on our way. Mr. Marchant and Mr. Athill were charmed with General Washington, who we found improved by retirement, like a Man relieved from an heavy burden. He had thrown off a little of that prudence which formerly guarded his every word, of course, He converses with the more ease and cheerfulness....

Philadelphia
12 July 1798
Washington has been named Commander in chief and agrees to accept.... Every thing here is Military and the Americans are actually carrying on War against France without the open declaration.

HENRIETTA LISTON

Philadelphia
17th Januy. 1799

In coming to Town this Winter We found
General Washington fixing, with the officers of
Government, the arrangements of the Army. He
dined with us one day, and called repeatedly, I
have scarcely ever seen a change of situation
produce a greater or more agreeable one in manners than in him. He was kind, affable, cheerful
and happy, and obtained a promise from us at
parting to visit him next summer....

Philadelphia
19th Decr. 1799

I write a few lines...to inform you of the Death
of George Washington.... Mr. Liston and I had
experienced such uniform politeness and friendly
attention from General Washington both while
President and after his retirement as to have
attached us warmly to him, and we feel extreme
satisfaction from having visited him so lately,
and parted from him so affectionately: It is difficult to say what may be the consequence of his
Death to this Country, He stood the barrier
between the Northernmost and Southernmost
States, He was Unenvied Head of the Army, and
such was the majic of his name that his opinion
was a sanction equal to law.—General
Washington was more the favourite of Fortune
than any Man in the World, He lived to see
accomplished every wish he had formed, and he
died at a moment when his life was as critically
necessary to his Country as at any preceding one.

JAMES MADISON
(1751-1836)

FOURTH PRESIDENT OF THE UNITED STATES

"...cool, considerate and cautious...."

In 1776, Madison helped draft the constitution of the new state of Virginia. He served in the legislature (1784-86) between his service in the Continental Congresses (1780-83 and 1787-88). With his keen understanding of constitutional law, Madison saw clearly the inherent weaknesses of the Articles of Confederation. Along with Alexander Hamilton's, his was the most forceful voice calling for a new constitutional convention. His hand was prominent in the drafting of the Constitution of the United States.

Madison, Hamilton, and John Jay wrote the influential Federalist Papers. He led the forces for adoption of the Constitution against the opposition of George Mason and Patrick Henry. As a member of Congress from 1789-97, he played a role in getting the new government on its feet and was a strong advocate for the first ten amendments to the Constitution, the Bill of Rights. In time, he became a staunch ally of Jefferson and an enemy of Hamilton.

When Jefferson was elected president in 1800, Madison became his secretary of state, serving throughout Jefferson's two terms. As president, beginning in 1809, he had to deal with the consequences of the foreign policy he had shaped. The nation gradually drifted toward the War of 1812 with Britain, with "war hawks" Henry Clay and John C. Calhoun clamoring for action.

The war was a mixture of battles won and lost. In 1814, British troops invaded and burned Washington. First Lady Dolley Madison rescued Gilbert Stuart's famous portrait of Washington before the British arrived to burn the President's House. The Treaty of Ghent ended the war later that year. In 1817, at the end of his second term, Madison and his wife retired to Montpelier, their estate in Virginia's Orange County.

There never was perhaps a greater contrast between two characters than between those of the President [Adams] and his predecessor [Washington].... The one cool, considerate and cautious, the other headlong and kindled into flame by every spark that lights on his passions; the one ever scrutinizing into the public opinion, and ready to follow where he could not lead it; the other insulting it by the most adverse sentiments and pursuits. Washington, a hero in the field, yet overweighing every danger in the Cabinet—Adams without a single pretension to the character of a soldier, a perfect Quixote as a statesman; the former Chief Magistrate pursuing peace everywhere with sincerity, though mistaking the means; the latter taking as much pains to get into war, as the former took to keep out of it....

—Letter to Thomas Jefferson, 1798, comparing Washington, in his first years of retirement, to Adams

The presidential mansion.

JAMES MADISON

GEORGE MASON

(1725-92)

STATESMAN, PATRIOT

*"...General Washington...is strongly attach'd to the Rights
& liberty of our country...."*

A wealthy Virginia planter, George Mason was also a
leader in the colony's public life. He was simultaneously
trustee of the town of Alexandria (1754-79), justice of the
Fairfax County court (until 1789), and vestryman of Truro
Parish (1748-85). In July 1775, he succeeded Washington in
the Virginia convention, an event that gave added impetus to
his growing opposition to British colonial policy. He had a
pivotal role in developing the state constitution and drafted
the Virginia Declaration of Rights. The latter document
served as a model for the other American colonies and influenced the formulation of the Declaration of Independence. In
1777, he was elected to the Continental Congress. In 1787,
he was a leading member of the Constitutional Convention

in Philadelphia. He took an active part in the drafting of the Constitution; however, he objected to the Convention's failure to include in it a Bill of Rights.

He objected also to what he saw as over-centralization of power and to compromises between New England and Southern states over slave and trade issues (he strongly opposed the perpetuation of slavery). He refused to sign the final document and, along with Patrick Henry, led a fight in Virginia against its ratification. He also declined a seat in the U.S. Senate, to which the Virginia legislature had elected him. Ultimately, he was vindicated with regard to one of his objections to the new Constitution: his draft Bill of Rights formed the basis of the first ten amendments to it.

In the new government there were frequent debates and arguments over interpretation of the Constitution. In the letter below, Mason expresses his concern over the surprise nomination of Gouverneur Morris, a monarchist sympathizer, to be ambassador to France. He writes, "I heard him [Morris] express the following sentiment: 'We must have a Monarch sooner or later' (tho' I think his word was a Despot), 'and the sooner we take him, while we are able to make a Bargain with him, the better.' Is this a man to represent the United States of America, in a Country, which has just reformed an arbitrary Monarchy into a free government?" Mason discusses at length the "advise and consent" role of the Senate with respect to ambassadorial nominees and gives this conclusion:

> I wish this important Subject to be fairly discussed, upon its merits, and decided upon, in the Infancy of the new Government, and in the presidency of General Washington, who, I am

GEORGE MASON

sure, is strongly attach'd to the Rights & liberty of our country, but we are not sure that this will be the Case with his Successors.

Letter to James Monroe,
written January 30, 1792, at Gunston Hall, Virginia

Washington's secretary and circular chair.

THE ESSENTIAL GEORGE WASHINGTON

GOUVERNEUR MORRIS

(1752-1816)

STATESMAN

"In him were the courage of a soldier, the intrepidity of a chief, the fortitude of a hero."

Born to a wealthy New York land-owning family loyal to the British crown, Morris in his youth was little interested in the growing tension between the colonies and the mother country. His half-brother, Lewis, was one of the signers of the Declaration of Independence, however, and, as a lawyer, Gouverneur was asked to be on a committee that drafted a constitution for the State of New York. He served in the Continental Congress from 1777 to 1780. Watching the soldiers at Valley Forge, Pennsylvania, during the winter of 1777, he was deeply impressed by their willingness to endure great hardships for the cause of freedom. He decided to join the effort, not as a soldier, but as an administrative aide to Washington. He served as an effective go-between for the commander in chief to Congress. After the war he settled in Philadelphia and became Pennsylvania delegate to the Constitutional Convention in 1787. He was a principal drafter of the Constitution, opening the introduction with the phrase "We the People of the United States...." A Federalist, he favored a strong central government, but realized that the Constitution would have to be flexible enough to suit unforeseeable circumstances, so some of his draft language was deliberately ambiguous. In 1792, he was appointed U.S. Minister to France. His sympathies lay with the royalists and he even participated in planning the attempted rescue of Louis XVI. From 1800-03, he was a U.S. senator from New York. He was a strong proponent of the Erie Canal.

Born to high destinies, he was fashioned for them by the hand of nature. His form was noble.... On his front were enthroned the virtues which exalt, and those which adorn the human character. So dignified his deportment, no man could approach him but with respect—none was great in his presence. His judgment was always clear, because his mind was pure. And seldom, if ever, will a sound understanding be met in the company of a corrupt heart.... In him were the courage of a soldier, the intrepidity of a chief, the fortitude of a hero.

—Quoted in "George Washington Bicentennial News," published by the Alexandria, Virginia, *Gazette* (Vol. 2, No. 2), November, 1932

NORDAMERICANISCHE KALENDAR

(1779)

GERMAN-LANGUAGE CALENDAR

"The Father of His Country."

Lancaster, Pennsylvania, printer Francis Baily was probably the first person to coin this phrase when he used it (as "Des Landes Vater") on a German-language calendar he published for the year 1779. In a letter to Washington on March 19, 1787, Secretary of War Henry Knox wrote, "Were an energetic and judicious system to be proposed with your signature it would be a circumstance highly honorable to your fame...and doubly entitle you to the glorious republican epithet, The Father of your Country." An editorial in the *Pennsylvania Packet* on July 9, 1789, carried the line, "The Father of His Country—We celebrate Washington!"

THOMAS PAINE
(1737-1809)

POLITICAL THEORIST, PAMPHLETEER

"The character and services of this gentleman are sufficient to put all those men called kings to shame."

Passionate and combative, Tom Paine become the chief propagandist for the American Revolution. Born in Thetford, Norfolk, England, this small, wiry son of a Quaker farmer and corset maker left school at thirteen to work for his father. Several jobs later, he became an excise tax collector. In 1772, he was dismissed after publishing a pamphlet agitating for higher salaries for excisemen as a means of ending corruption in the service. Meanwhile, he was studying on his own and had met Benjamin Franklin. In 1774, armed with a letter of introduction from Franklin, he sailed for America and landed a job as assistant editor of *Pennsylvania Magazine* in Philadelphia, a position he held from 1775-77. He also published articles anonymously, including one denouncing slavery. At the time he took up his editorial duties the colonies were divided over the issue of whether to declare independence from Great Britain.

On January 10, 1776, Paine's pamphlet *Common Sense* was published. It galvanized support for independence. He wrote, "Freedom has been hunted around the globe. Asia and Africa have expelled her...and England has given her warning to depart. O, receive the fugitive and prepare in time an asylum for mankind." Washington credited Paine with changing many minds from doubt to support for independence. In particular, *Common Sense* had a powerful effect on the men who created the Declaration of Independence. After the Declaration, he joined the Continental Army, seeing first hand the hardships being suffered by the ill-equipped troops. Public discouragement was widespread. In December 1776, Paine published the first of sixteen pamphlets in the series titled *The Crisis*. The first opened with the words "These are the times that try men's souls." Washington ordered it read to "every corporal's guard in the army."

Paine's passion and frankness would, however, ultimately get him into trouble. In 1781, he joined John Laurens's diplomatic mission to Paris, and in 1787 went on to London where he wrote *The Rights of Man,* attacking critics of the French Revolution (Member of Parliament Edmund Burke in particular) and English institutions in general. In this work Paine held up Washington as a model for monarchs to follow. This tome so angered British authorities that he was indicted for treason.

He fled to France, where he was elected to the National Convention. He argued, on humanitarian grounds, against the execution of Louis XVI, angering the Jacobins. Narrowly

THOMAS PAINE

escaping the guillotine himself, he was imprisoned in Paris in 1793. He languished there for ten months before James Monroe, then United States ambassador, and other American friends secured his release.

In 1794-96, deeply affected by the French Revolution, Paine wrote *The Age of Reason,* in which he attacked organized religion and extolled Deism, the belief in a God who exerts no influence on the actions of individuals. His once-widespread popularity with the American public evaporated. Washington's friends, in particular, turned their backs on him after he wrote a scathing and bitter letter, blaming Washington for insufficient effort to extricate him from his French prison sentence. Paine returned to the United States in 1802, ostracized. His health began to fail, and in 1809 he died an outcast in New York City.

> The character and services of this gentleman are sufficient to put all those men called kings to shame. While they are receiving from the sweat and labors of mankind a prodigality of pay to which neither their abilities nor their services can entitle them, he is rendering every service in his power, and refusing every pecuniary reward. He accepted no pay as commander-in-chief; he accepts none as President of the United States.
>
> —From *Rights of Man,* 1791-92

As to you, sir, treacherous to private friendship (for so you have been to me, and that in the day of danger) and a hypocrite in public life, the world will be puzzled to decide whether you are an apostate or an impostor, whether you have abandoned good principles or whether you ever had any.

—Letter to Washington, July 30, 1796

View of Mount Vernon.

THOMAS PAINE

THE PHILADELPHIA
FEDERAL GAZETTE

NEWSPAPER

"...our saviour and our guide."

On April 24, 1789, the *Federal Gazette* published a poem lauding Washington, and submitted, in French, by a reader. The editor requested "some ingenious correspondent to favor him with a translation." A Philadelphia gentlemen supplied the version below:

G eneral! immortalized by virtuous fame!
E ngland's brave foe! to France how dear thy name!
O 'er our young Senate hasten to preside;
R ule a glad land; our saviour and our guide.
G overn by law; and shew admiring men
(E nvy may howl) OUR noblest citizen.
W ise, valiant! may thy name still brighter grow;
A nd make mankind to worth and virtue bow;
S teady in justice to thyself and friends;
H appy that people, which thy worth commends.
I nstruction shall descend from sires to sons;
N o name so great, so dear, as Washington's.
G enerous and just! we dread from thee no wrong;
T hy gallant deeds have silenc'd Envy's tongue.
O ! to the warrior's add the statesman's praise,
N or scorn once more a drooping land to raise.

—Edition of August 30, 1789

ELIZABETH POWEL

WASHINGTON FAMILY FRIEND

*"God alone could have blended the great,
good & amiable in one Mortal."*

Elizabeth Powel and her husband, Samuel, the mayor of Philadelphia, were close friends of the Washingtons. Upon General Washington's retirement from command of the army, Mrs. Powel wrote her thoughts about him in a letter to a friend, Mrs. William Fitzhugh.

Philadelphia
December 24, 1783

Few in his situation, after having so successfully played a Game for their Country but would have played an after-Game for themselves; but in the Estimation of all wise & good Men, he will be more glorious in his Retirement than he ever was when in the Zenith of his Power. God alone could have blended the great, good & amiable in one Mortal. He, in the most eminent Degree, possesses the inflexible Virtues of a Cato, the Graces of Caesar, the Valor of a Scipio, the Piety of an Oneas & the Humility & Moderation of a Cincinnatus. A moderation that I sincerely hope will make him eventually more happy than the greatest Monarch of the most extensive Empire can ever be.... Virginia has the exclusive Honor of giving birth & Education to a greater Hero than ancient or modern Times can boast. When you see him, present my most friendly Wishes for his Health & Happiness. The inhabitants of Philadelphia parted with him with regret, & will ever receive him with Gratitude & Pleasure.

ELIZABETH POWEL

JOHN ROBINSON

SPEAKER OF THE VIRGINIA HOUSE OF BURGESSES, 1759

"...your modesty is equal to your valor...."

To aid in fighting the French and Indian War, Virginia raised its own army with an authorization of up to two thousand men. In 1754, Washington, then twenty-two, was elected "Colonel of the Virginia Regiment and Commander in Chief of all Virginia forces." Although he had self-doubts as to his ability to carry out the assignment, his reputation was at stake, so he sought complete control over selection of officers and procurement of supplies. The House of Burgesses was happy to hand him full authority—and responsibility. He selected men he felt were the most able, not only those with impeccable pedigrees, and was rewarded with their intense loyalty. His experience prepared him for the difficulties that lay a few years in the future, in the Revolutionary War. Supplying his Virginia regiment was a constant nightmare, requiring great ingenuity and attention to detail on

Washington's part. Following Braddock's defeat and death in 1755 (when Washington was lauded by his fellow-colonials for advising Braddock to fight Indian-style), the regiment had the unenviable task of defending scattered homesteads in the Shenandoah Valley. During the years 1755-59, Washington's treatment by high-handed British military commanders undoubtedly contributed to his growing alienation from the Crown. Finally, in November 1758, he and his troops were with the British Army regulars near Fort Duquesne seeking to take the fort that eluded Braddock. To their surprise, they found the French had burned the fort and disappeared from the area. Peace was secured for the frontier. Thinking his military career was at an end, Washington resigned his commission and returned to Mount Vernon. A grateful House of Burgesses met in the capital, Williamsburg, to thank him for his service. Rising to respond, Washington found himself speechless.

Sit down, Mr. Washington; your modesty is equal to your valor, and that surpasses the power of any language that I possess.

JOHN ROBINSON

GILBERT STUART
(1755-1828)

PORTRAIT PAINTER

*"All his features were indicative
of the strongest passions...."*

Stuart showed an early talent for drawing and ultimately became the leading American painter of the day. He followed Scotsman Cosmo Alexander, his first teacher, to Edinburgh, but returned upon Alexander's death. In 1775 he went to London, supporting himself as an organist and by way of occasional portrait commissions. He came to the attention of the famous Benjamin West and became his pupil. This led to his being exhibited at the Royal Academy of Arts for most of the years from 1777 to 1785. It was his "Portrait of a Gentleman Skating" (1782) which gained him fame and a steady clientele. He was nevertheless in debt because of extravagant living. In 1787, he moved to Dublin, where he gained a new following. As a means of achieving lasting solvency, he conceived the idea of painting a portrait of Washington, then making replicas for sale. He returned to America in 1792, settling in Philadelphia and later in Boston (1805). He painted three portraits of Washington from life, making fifteen replicas of the first and seventy-five of the third. He also painted portraits of Jefferson, Madison, and Monroe, and of his fellow painters, West, John Singleton Copley, and Sir Joshua Reynolds, among others.

There were features in his face totally different from what I had observed in any other human being.... All his features were indicative of the strongest passions; yet like Socrates his judgment and self-command made him appear a man of different cast in the eyes of the world.

—c. 1797, quoted in James Thomas Flexner's
Gilbert Stuart (1955)

GILBERT STUART

EDWARD THORNTON
(1766-1852)

British diplomat

*"I promised you...a description of the
President of the United States...."*

The son of a London innkeeper, Edward Thornton was orphaned at an early age. He was given a scholarship at Pembroke College, Cambridge. He then sought a patron to help him on a career path. In 1789 he became tutor to the sons of James Bland Burges, a member of Parliament and undersecretary to the secretary of state for the Foreign Department, the Duke of Leeds. Thornton became a favorite of the Burges family and this led to his appointment as secretary to George Hammond, the newly appointed minister to the United States (diplomatic relations had been normalized in 1791). Hammond, the son of a leading Yorkshire landowner, was only three years older than Thornton. The two left for America in fall 1791. Before departing, Burges asked Thornton to write to him often, which the latter did on a personal level, outside his formal official reports. Hammond and Thornton found that most of the other major powers were well advanced in developing their relationships with the young U.S. government. Secretary of State Thomas Jefferson was anxious that Britain make a commercial agreement with the U.S., as most of the other countries had done. Also, implementation of the Treaty of Paris had yet to be resolved. The two Britons found also a circle of Anglophiles, headed by Alexander Hamilton. In 1793, with England and France again at war, Thornton was dispatched to Baltimore as vice-consul. He returned to England in 1799. Back again in 1801, he acted as chargé d'affaires through 1803. His letters to Burges are remarkable for their candor and scope, giving his patron a detailed picture of the character and outlook of American leaders. His views of Washington range from respect and admiration to boredom, skepticism, even cynicism. Doubtless they were colored in part by Washington's age (sixty), Thornton's youth (twenty-six) and the latter's allegiance to the Crown.

Philadelphia
April 2, 1792

I promised you in a former letter a description of the President of the United States, conscious as I am of the difficulty...of describing again what has been so often described before, I will yet attempt to convey to you my idea of him. His person is tall and sufficiently graceful, his face well-formed, his complexion rather pale, with a mild and philosophic gravity in the expression of it. In his air and manner he displays much natural dignity, in his address he is cold, reserved and even phlegmatic, though with-

EDWARD THORNTON

out the least appearance of haughtiness and ill nature; it is the effect I imagine of constitutional diffidence. That caution and circumspection which form so striking and well-known a feature in his military and indeed in his political character, is very strongly marked in his countenance: for his eyes retire inward (do you understand me?) and have nothing of fire, of animation or openness in their expression. If this circumspection is accompanied by discernment and penetration, as I am informed it is, and as I should be inclined to believe from the judicious choice he has generally made of persons to fill public stations, he possesses the two great requisites of a statesman, the faculty of concealing his own sentiments, and of discovering those of other men. A certain degree of indecision however, a want of vigour and energy may be observed in some of his actions, and are indeed the obvious result of too refined caution. He is a man of great but secret ambition, and has sometimes, I think condescended to use little arts, and those too very shallow ones, to secure the object of that ambition. He is, I am told, indefatigable in business and extremely clear and systematic in the arrangement of it; his time is regularly divided into certain portions, and the business allotted to any one portion rigidly attended to. Of his private character, I can say very little positive; I have never heard of any truly noble, generous or disinterested action of his; he has very few, who are on terms of intimate and unreserved friendship; and what is worse, he is less beloved in his own state (Virginia) than in any part of the

United States. After all, he is a great man; circumstances have made him so; but I cannot help
thinking that the misconduct of our commanders
has given him a principle part of that greatness.
It does not resemble (to conclude this description
with a simile) that of the mid-day sun, of which
we form a magnificent idea from its owns
irresistible brightness and invigorating heat; but
it is that of a setting sun, whose magnitude is
increased from the confused and misty atmos-
phere that surrounds it.

Philadelphia
June 11, 1792
I have been honoured by an invitation to dine
with him [Washington]. Except in the honor,
believe me there is nothing pleasant in the circumstance: for it is of all others the most dull
and unentertaining. The President's reserve, the
affect partly I think of pride, partly of constitutional diffidence, throws a restraint on the whole
party. The conversation in consequence (was)
unanimously phlegmatic and trivial....

Philadelphia
October 3, 1792
Mr. Hammond returned on Sunday last from a
short excursion for a week or ten days as far as
Mount Vernon, the seat of the President in
Virginia. He speaks in high terms of the grandeur
of the country through which he passed, and
especially of that part on the banks of the
Potomack in the neighborhood of Mount
Vernon. The President is a great farmer, and

EDWARD THORNTON

delights much in agricultural pursuits; indeed I
am told that he feels more animation and throws
off more of his natural phlegm when conversing
on that topic than on any other. When I tell you
that he will raise this year from his lands nine
thousand bushels of wheat, you will allow that
he is a farmer of no contemptible scale. His pro-
ductive estate, which I have heard estimated at
about five thousand pounds per annum, is situat-
ed along the banks of the Potomack about fifteen
miles or more below the site of the future federal
city. I would not willingly attribute improper
motives to great eagerness in any pursuit; but the
accession of value to his property will be considerable from the circumstances of the permanent
seat of government being in his neighborhood, so
that one cannot entirely give him credit for perfect disinterestedness or attribute his ardor for
attainment of this object to the purest motives.
Mr. Hammond says that the site of the federal
city is extremely grand, and it is certainly well
imagined as to its central position....

Philadelphia
March 5, 1793
I was present yesterday at the ceremony of
administering the oath of office to Mr.
Washington on his re-election for the next four
years as President of the United States. It was
administered by one of the Judges of the
Supreme Court in the Senate Chamber in the
presence of the Senators and as many individuals
as could be crowded into the room. The
President first made a short speech, expressive of

his sense of high honor conferred upon him by his re-election. There was nothing particular in the ceremony itself.

Our innovating demagogues in England will, I suppose, draw strong inferences in favor of the electing of the first executive magistrate from this instance which is certainly an uncommon one, of an unanimous choice of the whole people repeated in his favor. I confess I am not disposed to consider this circumstance as so highly honorable to the object of it, as others might be who take a slight view of it. I consider it rather as a mutual concession of prejudices on the part of the people than as the unanimous acknowledgement of incontestable superiority of merit; and as far as it is honorable to have conciliated opposite tempers and suppressed partial dislikes, I allow that credit to the President. The circumstance which proves incontestably I think, that I am right in this opinion, is that a great number of votes for Vice-President [John Adams], his second and in certain events his successor, was given to a man whose principles are diametrically opposite to those of the President, and who has been and still is the decided opponent of the measures of the present government and of the federal constitution itself. This conduct can be explained on no ground I think but either of most strange inconsistency or the kind of mutual concession which I mention. After all, it must be said that he is man in the whole continent for whom such concessions would be made....

EDWARD THORNTON

MARTHA DANDRIDGE WASHINGTON

(1731-1802)

WIFE OF GEORGE WASHINGTON

*"It was with very great pleasure I see...
you got safely down."*

Martha Washington, the daughter of John and Frances Dandridge, was considered a charming beauty among the Virginia aristocracy when she married Daniel Park Custis in 1749. She bore him four children (two of whom died in childhood), and his death in 1757 left her one of the richest women in Virginia. George Washington met her early the next year and proposed not many months afterward. They were married in January 1759. He took Martha and her surviving children—Martha Parke Custis (d. 1773) and John Parke Custis (d. 1781)—to live at Mount Vernon. The couple had no children of their own, but after John Custis died, Washington adopted two of his four children: Eleanor Parke Custis and George Washington Park Custis (whose daughter married Robert E. Lee). Martha and George Washington were deeply devoted to each other. For nearly half a century, she was noted for her graciousness as the hostess of Mount Vernon. The letter quoted here was prompted by concern for her husband's safety in a journey over muddy, hazardous roads to Williamsburg to attend a session of the House of Burgesses.

March 30, 1767
My Dearest,

It was with very great pleasure I see in your letter that you got safely down. We are all very well at this time, but it is still rainney and wett. I am sorry you will not be at home soon, as I expected you. I had rather my sister would not come up so soon, as May would be a much plasenter time than April. We wrote you last post; as I have nothing new to tell you, I must conclude myself.

Your Most Affectionate
Martha Washington

MASON LOCKE WEEMS
(1759-1825)

PREACHER, FIRST WASHINGTON BIOGRAPHER

"I can't tell a lie, Pa."

Born in Virginia, Parson Weems studied theology in London, was ordained in 1784 and served as rector of several Episcopal parishes, including Washington's Mount Vernon (Pohick Church). He was also for many years a traveling sales agent for Matthew Carey, a Philadelphia publisher and book seller. He is best known as Washington's first biographer, with *The Life and Memorable Actions of George Washington* (c. 1800), which went through some forty editions. Beginning with the fifth edition, it included the famous cherry-tree story. In his effort to immortalize Washington, Weems had the six-year-old George chopping down a young cherry tree. According to Weems, the boy's father said, "George, do you know who killed that beautiful little cherry tree yonder in the garden?" Weems wrote that this was "a tough question and George staggered under it for a moment." After the confession, the father says, "Run to my arms, you dearest boy; run to my arms; glad am I, George, that you killed my tree, for you have paid me for it a thousand fold. Such an act of heroism in my son is worth more than a thousand trees, though blossomed with silver, and their fruits of purest gold." Although Washington was well known for his honesty, there is no factual basis for the Weems story. Weems also wrote biographies of William Penn and Benjamin Franklin, and a pamphlet entitled "The Drunkard's Looking-glass," which he sold in taverns throughout the South after first getting the patrons' attention by imitating the actions of a drunk.

I can't tell a lie, Pa; you know I can't tell a lie. I did cut it with my hatchet.

—From *The Life and Memorable Actions of George Washington* (c. 1800)

MASON LOCKE WEEMS

PART II

BETWEEN THEN
AND NOW

GEORGE GORDON, LORD BYRON

(1788-1824)

BRITISH POET

"...the first—the last—the best—
The Cincinnatus of the West...."

Byron, Keats, and Shelley are thought of as the greatest British Romantic poets of the first half of the nineteenth century. In their day, Byron was the most famous of the trio. His father, "Mad Jack" Byron, an army officer, died when Byron was three, leaving the boy and his mother in poverty. Born with a deformed foot, about which he was very sensitive, young George was alternately the subject of his mother's excessive tenderness and her uncontrolled temper.

When he was ten, he inherited the baronetcy of his great uncle and moved into the dilapidated family castle, Newstead

Abbey. He later graduated from Cambridge, concentrating on literature. To compensate for his disability he became a good swimmer, boxer, marksman, and horseback rider. In 1808, he took up his seat in the House of Lords. In his first speech, in 1812, he championed the cause of weavers thrown out of work by the invention of power looms. He was immediately seen by his peers as a revolutionary. Meanwhile, his collection of poems, *House of Idleness* (1807), was attacked by the *Edinburgh Review.* He responded with the satiric *English Bards and Scotch Reviewers* and gained immediate fame.

Handsome, and a stylish dresser, Byron attracted a great following among women. In 1815, he married Anne Isabella Milbanke, but they were separated the next year (probably over scandalous rumors about his being in an incestuous relationship with his half-sister). An outcast socially, he left England, never to return. In 1819 he took up with Countess Teresa Guiccioli, who remained his mistress for the rest of his life.

In Europe, he wrote his most famous lyric poems, *Childe Harold* and *Manfred,* and a verse play, *Don Juan.* In his last two years, he devoted himself to the cause of Greek independence from the Turks of the Ottoman Empire. The life of action he sought was at hand when he caught a fever in Greece and died. His admiration for heroic men of action was captured in his lines about George Washington.

LORD BYRON

Where may the wearied eye repose
   When gazing on the Great,
Where neither guilty glory glows,
   Nor despicable state?

Yes—one—the first—the last—the best—
The Cincinnatus of the West,
   Whom envy dared not hate,
Bequeath'd the name of Washington,
To make man blush there was but one?

—From *Ode to Napoleon,* 1814

While Washington's a watchword, such as ne'er
Shall sink while there's an echo left to air...

—From *The Age of Bronze,* 1823

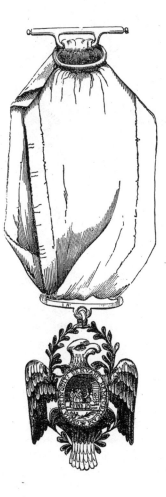

Medal of the Order of the Cincinnati,
a fraternity of Revolutionary War officers.

JAMES FENIMORE COOPER
(1789-1851)

NOVELIST

"They may talk of their Jeffersons...."

When he was a year old, Cooper's family moved to Cooperstown, founded by his father, on the shores of New York's Lake Otsego. He entered Yale at age thirteen, but three years later was expelled for misbehavior. He then spent five years at sea, the last three as a midshipman in the U.S. Navy. His first novel was a failure, but his second, *The Spy* (1821), set in the American Revolution, was an immediate success. For the rest of his life he was fully occupied as a writer with a large following. In 1826, he was appointed U.S. consul in Lyon, France. While there, he wrote *Notions of the Americans* (1836) in defense of his countrymen. After his return to the United States, he wrote in 1838 a series of criticisms of his own country that made him unpopular (*Home as Found*, the fictional sequel to *Homeward Bound* and *The*

American Democrat). His most popular books were the Leatherstocking Tales, named for their fictional hero, frontiersman Natty Bumppo, also known as "Leatherstocking." All the stories were set in frontier days: *The Pioneers, The Last of the Mohicans, The Prairie, The Pathfinder,* and *The Deerslayer.* He also wrote several popular novels of the sea and a highly regarded *History of the United States Navy* (1839). He was proudest of his creation Natty Bumppo and was not modest in praising him.

They may talk of their Jeffersons and Jacksons, but I set down Washington and Natty Bumppo as the two only really great men of my time.

—From *Home As Found* (1838)

JAMES FENIMORE COOPER

ANN PAMELA CUNNINGHAM

(1816-75)

SAVIOR OF MOUNT VERNON

"Oh, it cannot be possible!"

As a young woman living near Charleston, South Carolina, Ann Pamela Cunningham was severely injured in a horseback-riding accident and became a semi-invalid. During her convalescence, her mother visited relatives in Washington, D.C., and returned home by boat. As the boat glided down the Potomac, the mother spied Mount Vernon. Her excitement turned to shock, for George Washington's home was going to ruin. Columns were missing from the portico, the roof was in disrepair, the grounds overgrown. When this was related to Ann Pamela, she decided to make the rescue of Mount Vernon her life's work.

On hearing rumors that Washington's estate might be sold to Northern interests as a factory site, she was appalled and launched her campaign with an open letter to "The Ladies of the South" in a local newspaper. Following this, she mounted a concerted effort to enlist the aid of political, business, and civic leaders and historians to raise the money to buy Mount Vernon.

Finally, in 1858, Miss Cunningham and her band of women volunteers had the funds to purchase Mount Vernon. Restoration work began at once, but was suspended during the Civil War. She obtained the agreement of both sides to treat Mount Vernon as neutral ground, a promise that was kept. Indeed, soldiers on leave from both sides visited the estate throughout the war. After the war, restoration work resumed and continues to this day. The Mount Vernon Ladies' Association, which Miss Cunningham headed for twenty-one years, is governed by an all-woman council, headed by a regent. Each of thirty-two states is represented by a vice regent. By the terms of its by-laws, Mount Vernon accepts no government funds.

Can you be still with closed souls and purses while the world cries "Shame upon America," and suffer Mount Vernon, with all its sacred associations, to become, as is spoken of and probable, the seat of manufacturing...noise and smoke, and the "busy hum of men," destroying all sanctity and repose around the tomb of your own "world's wonder"? Oh, it cannot be possible!

WASHINGTON, and his principles and spirit, appear no longer to influence the City which bears his name. Oh! who that have a spark of patriotism, but must mourn such early degeneracy,

ANN PAMELA CUNNINGHAM

when they see who fill our Legislative halls and crowd our political Metropolis!

One of your countrywomen feels emboldened to appeal in the name of the Mother of Washington, and of Southern feeling and honor, to all that is sympathetic and generous in your nature, to exert itself, and by your combined effort now, in village and country, town and city, the means may be raised from the mites of thousands of gentle hearts, upon whom his name has yet a magic spell, which will suffice to secure and retain his home and grave as a SACRED SPOT for all coming times.

A spontaneous work like this would be such a monument of love and gratitude, as has never yet been reared to purest patriot and mortal man; and while it would save American honor from a blot in the eyes of a gazing world, it would furnish a shrine where at least the mothers of the land and their indignant children, might make their offerings in the cause of greatness, goodness, and prosperity of their country.

A Southern Matron

—From "To the Ladies of the South," published in the *Charleston Mercury,* December 2, 1853

George Washington as a Virginia colonel at the age of forty.

DAVID DAVIS
(1815-86)

U.S. SUPREME COURT JUSTICE, U.S. SENATOR

"Wicked men...may fill the place...."

In 1836, David Davis settled in Bloomington, Illinois, to practice law. From 1848 to 1862 he presided over the state's Eighth Judicial Circuit, often traveling the circuit with his good friend Abraham Lincoln, who practiced before that court. Davis was instrumental in securing for Lincoln the Republican nomination for president in 1860. In 1862, Lincoln appointed him to the U.S. Supreme Court, where he wrote one of the most important opinions in the court's history: Ex Parte Milligan, which buttressed civil liberties. In 1877, he resigned from the court to become the U.S. senator from Illinois (1877-83).

Our nation has no right to expect that it will always have wise and humane rulers, sincerely attached to the principles of the Constitution. Wicked men, ambitious of power, with hatred of liberty and law, may fill the place once occupied by Washington and Lincoln.

—From an opinion written in the case
of Ex Parte Mulligan, 1866

DAVID DAVIS

RALPH WALDO EMERSON
(1803-82)

POET AND ESSAYIST

*"[It is] as if this man had absorbed
all the serenity of America."*

The son of a Unitarian minister, Emerson had a brief career as a clergyman, but his belief in the primacy of the individual led him instead to a literary life. Two lectures at Harvard, in 1837 and 1838, gained him wide attention. In one, he called for American independence from European culture. In the other he asserted that one could find redemption only in one's own soul—a highly controversial view. He had regular lecture tours in the 1840s and 1850s, often expressing anti-slavery views. He resided in Concord, Massachusetts.

The head of Washington hangs in my dining-room for a few days past, and I cannot keep my eyes off of it. It has a certain Appalachian strength, as if it were truly the first-fruits of America, and expressed the Country. The heavy, leaden eyes turn on you, as the eyes of an ox in a pasture. And the mouth has gravity and depth of quiet, as if this MAN had absorbed all the serenity of America, and left none for his restless, rickety, hysterical countrymen.

—From *The Journals of Ralph Waldo Emerson* (1852)

RALPH WALDO EMERSON

EDWARD EVERETT

(1794-1865)

STATESMAN, ORATOR

"The character...of...Washington...
will guide our children...."

On finishing his degrees at Harvard in 1814, Everett became a Unitarian minister. The following year he was appointed a professor of Greek literature at Harvard. During his ten-year professorship he traveled widely and also edited the *North American Review.* In 1824, he was elected to the U.S. House of Representatives and served for five terms. He was governor of Massachusetts (1836-39), U.S. minister to England (1841-45), and president of Harvard (1846-49). In late 1852, in the final months of the Millard Fillmore administration, he succeeded his friend Daniel Webster as secretary of state. By then, he had been elected as U.S. senator for Massachusetts; he resigned the seat in 1854, however, facing growing opposition to his Whig views on slavery, which called for compromise with the South. During the Civil War, he traveled extensively through the North, championing the Union cause. A skilled orator, he drew huge crowds. On November 19, 1863, he was invited to give the principal address at the dedication of the Gettysburg, Pennsylvania, battlefield cemetery. His hour-long speech is forgotten today, while President Abraham Lincoln's brief Gettysburg Address endures as one of the noblest public speeches ever given.

The character, the counsels, and example of our Washington...will guide us through the doubts and difficulties that beset us; they will guide our children and our children's children in the paths of prosperity and peace, while America shall hold her place in the family of nations.

—From the speech, "Washington Abroad and at Home,"
July 5, 1858

EDWARD EVERETT

PAUL von HINDENBURG

(1847-1934)

GERMAN PRESIDENT, FIELD MARSHAL

*"George Washington...belongs among
the immortals of world history."*

By age thirty-one, Hindenburg's military career had been so successful that he was appointed to the Prussian Army's general staff. In World War I, coming out of retirement to head the German Army on the Eastern front, he led a major victory over a much larger Russian force. In 1917, he led German forces on the Western front, but the Allies, augmented by the infusion of American troops, turned back the German offensive, winning the war. A monarchist, he was elected president of the Reich in 1925. In 1932, in an ad hoc coalition with the Socialists, he defeated Hitler in the presidential election. Later that year, probably suffering the effects of senility, he turned against the Socialists, persuaded they were plotting against the government. In early 1933, he appointed Hitler as chancellor, inadvertently opening the door for the march of Nazism. Hindenburg, though in his dotage, remained as figurehead president until his death.

In connection with the celebration of the 200th anniversary of the birth of your great national hero, George Washington, who was a model leader of his fellow countrymen in war and peace, belongs among the immortals of the world's history....Washington's strong hand steered the young American ship of state safely through all reefs during a most difficult period.

—Letter to the President of the United States, February 22, 1932, during the bicentennial year commemoration of Washington's birth

PAUL VON HINDENBURG

OLIVER WENDELL HOLMES, SR.

(1809-94)

PHYSICIAN, POET, ESSAYIST

"Not for him an earthly crown!"

While Holmes was studying law at Harvard, his first poem, "Old Ironsides," was published. He soon shifted his study to medicine, later becoming a professor of anatomy at Dartmouth and then Harvard, where he became dean of the medical school (1847-53). He also wrote several important medical papers. He was a popular lecturer with his students and on the general lecture circuit. In 1857, he began a series of articles for the *Atlantic Monthly,* which were later published as a series of books: *The Autocrat of the Breakfast-Table* (1858), *The Professor of the Breakfast-Table* (1860), *The Poet of the Breakfast-Table* (1872) and *Over the Teacups* (1891). His wit and his gift for rhyming made him a popular poet. His son, Oliver Wendell Holmes, Jr., served as an associate justice of the United States Supreme Court (1902-32).

Vain is empire's mad temptation!
Not for him an earthly crown!
He whose sword hath freed a nation
Strikes the offered sceptre down.
See the throneless Conqueror seated,
Ruler by a people's choice;
See the Patriot's task completed;
Hear the Father's dying voice.

"By the name that you inherit,
By the sufferings you recall,
Cherish the fraternal spirit;
Love your country first of all!
Listen not to idle questions
If its bands may be untied;
Doubt the patriot whose suggestions
Strive a nation to divide!"

Father! We, whose ears have tingled
With the discord-notes of shame, —
Gathering, while this holy morning
Lights the land from sea to sea,
Hear thy counsel, heed thy warning;
Trust us, while we honor thee!

—From "Ode for Washington's Birthday," given at the
Celebration of the Mercantile Library Association,
Boston, February 24, 1856

OLIVER WENDELL HOLMES, SR.

ABRAHAM LINCOLN
(1809-65)

SIXTEENTH PRESIDENT OF THE UNITED STATES, 1861-65

"Washington is the mightiest name on earth...."

By the time Lincoln gave this Washington's Birthday speech, he was at the end of his four terms as an Illinois state legislator. He had a thriving law partnership in Springfield and was beginning to gain a reputation for lucidity and eloquence in his public addresses. He was just thirty-three years old. Like Washington, Lincoln had little formal schooling, but thirsted for knowledge. Like Washington, his character became highly regarded—for honesty, sincerity, and capability. And, like Washington, in death his life and accomplishments became legendary.

Washington is the mightiest name on earth—long since mightiest in the cause of civil liberty, still mightiest in moral reformation. On that name no eulogy is expected. It can not be. To add brightness to the sun, or glory to the name of Washington is alike impossible. Let none attempt it. In solemn awe we pronounce the name, and in its naked deathless splendor leave it shining on.

—From an address in Springfield, Illinois, February 22, 1842

ABRAHAM LINCOLN

HENRY CABOT LODGE, SR.

(1850-1924)

U.S. SENATOR

*"He learned to know these men and they came
to love, obey and follow him...."*

Henry Cabot Lodge, Sr., is remembered today as Woodrow Wilson's nemesis in the latter's effort to get the United States to join the League of Nations. As a senator, Lodge led the opposition to the 1919 Treaty of Versailles and to the League. Less well known are his earlier careers as editor (the *North American Review*, the *International Review*), Harvard University lecturer, and published historian. He held bachelor's, law, and doctoral degrees from Harvard. He wrote four biographies: of his great-grandfather, George Cabot (1877), Alexander Hamilton (1882), Daniel Webster (1883) and George Washington (1889). He also edited the complete works of Hamilton (1885).

When he first went among the New England troops at the siege of Boston, the rough, democratic ways of the people jarred upon him, and offended especially his military instincts, for he was not only a Virginian, but he was a soldier, and military discipline is essentially aristocratic. These volunteer soldiers, called together from the plough and the fishing-smack, were free and independent men, unaccustomed to any rule but their own, and they had still to learn the first rudiments of military service. To Washington, soldiers who elected and deposed their officers, and who went home when they felt that they had right to do so, seemed well-nigh useless and almost incomprehensible. They angered him and tried his patience almost beyond endurance, and he spoke of them at the outset in harsh terms by no means wholly unwarranted. But they were part of his problem, and he studied them. He was a soldier, but not an aristocrat wrapped up in immutable prejudices, and he learned to know these men, and they came to love, obey and follow him with an intelligent devotion far better than anything born of discipline. They stayed with him till the end.

—From Volume II of *George Washington* (1889)

HENRY CABOT LODGE, SR.

BENSON J. LOSSING

(1813-91)

HISTORIAN

"I lingered long at the tomb of Washington...."

Orphaned as a boy and self-taught, Benson Lossing became an immensely popular historian following publication of his *Pictorial Field Book of the Revolution,* first as a series of pamphlets (1850-52), then as a two-volume set (1859). To research this work, Lossing traveled eight thousand miles, covering the sites of the Revolution, interviewing survivors (and two U.S. presidents), and visiting battlefields, historic buildings, and Washington's tomb.

A skilled engraver—as a teenager he had been apprenticed to a watchmaker and later established a successful engraving business in New York City—Lossing drew hundreds of sketches to illustrate his volumes. His writing style and illustrations made American history readily accessible to the general public. He followed this success with similar books on the War of 1812 and the Civil War; he wrote and illustrated some forty titles of history and biography.

In the ante-chamber of the tomb are two marble sarcophagi containing the remains of Washington and his lady. That of the patriot has a sculptured lid on which is represented the American shield suspended over the flag of the Union; the latter hung in festoons and the whole surmounted, as a crest, by an eagle of open wings, perched upon the superior bar of the shield. Below the design, and deeply cut in the marble, is the name, "WASHINGTON." This sarcophagus was constructed by John Struthers of Philadelphia from a design by William Strickland and presented by him to the relatives of Washington. It consists of an excavation from a single block of Pennsylvania marble, eight feet in length and two in height. The marble coffin of Lady Washington, which stands upon the left of the other, is from the same chisel and plainly wrought.

Who can stand at the portals of this tomb, where sleeps all that remains of the mortality of the Father of his Country, and not feel the devotional spirit—an involuntary desire to kneel down with reverence, not with the false adulations of mere hero worship, but with the sincere sympathies of a soul bending before the shrine of superior goodness and greatness?

BENSON J. LOSSING

I lingered long at the tomb of Washington, even until the lengthening evening shadows were cast upon the Potomac; and I departed with reluctance from the precincts of Mount Vernon, where the great and good of many lands enjoyed the hospitality of the illustrious owner when living, or have poured forth the silent eulogium of the heart at his grave.

—From *Pictorial Field Book of the Revolution,* Vol. II
(1859)

Washington's tomb.

JAMES RUSSELL LOWELL
(1819-91)

POET, ESSAYIST, EDITOR, DIPLOMAT

"...he towered above them all..."

Lowell studied law at Harvard, graduating in 1841. Poetry, however, was his first love, and that same year his first volume of poems was published. He also founded a magazine that year, thus beginning a long career as editor or contributor to many periodicals. His reputation as a wit and satirist was established in 1846 with publication of *Biglow Papers* a Yankee vernacular criticism of the Mexican War. A second series of *Biglow Papers* was published in 1862-67 on Civil War issues. In 1856, he succeeded Henry Wadsworth Longfellow as professor of Spanish and French at Harvard, a post he held for twenty years. Meanwhile, he became the first editor of the *Atlantic Monthly,* and later of the *North American Review*. Several collections of his essays on English authors were published as books. Among his poems, *Three*

Memorial Poems (on Washington, Lincoln, and America) were highly regarded. In 1877, he was appointed by President Rutherford B. Hayes as minister to Spain. Three years later he was named minister to Great Britain, where he lived until 1885. He did much to increase appreciation, in Spain and Britain, for American letters and institutions. His speeches given in England were published in 1887 under the title *Democracy and Other Addresses.*

Beneath our consecrated elm
A century ago he stood,
Famed vaguely for that old fight in the wood
Whose red surge sought, but could not overwhelm
The life foredoomed to wield our rough-hewn helm:—
From colleges, where now the gown
To arms had yielded, from the town,
Our rude self-summoned levies flocked to see
The new-come chiefs and wonder which was he.
No need to question long; close-lipped and tall,
Long trained in murder-brooding forests lone
To bridle others' clamors and his own,
Firmly erect, he towered above them all,
The incarnate discipline that was to free
With iron curb that armed democracy.

* * *

Soldier and statesman, rarest unison;
High-poised example of great duties done
Simply as breathing, a world's honors worn
As life's indifferent gifts to all men born;
Dumb for himself, unless it were to God,

But for his barefoot soldiers eloquent,
Tramping the snow to coral where they trod,
Held by his awe in hollow-eyed content;
Modest, yet firm as Nature's self; unblamed
Save by the men his nobler temper shamed;
Never seduced through show of present good
By other than unsetting lights to steer
New-trimmed in Heaven, nor than his steadfast
    mood
More steadfast, far from rashness as from fear;
Rigid, but with himself first, grasping still
In swerveless poise the wave-beat helm of will;
Not honored then or now because he wooed
The popular voice, but that he still withstood;
Broad-minded, higher-souled, there is but one
Who was all this and ours, and all men's
    —WASHINGTON.

—From "Under the Old Elm" in the collection
Three Memorial Poems (1875)

JAMES RUSSELL LOWELL

HENRY DAVID THOREAU
(1817-62)

NATURALIST, ESSAYIST, POET

"He could advance and he could withdraw."

Twice a resident in Ralph Waldo Emerson's household, Thoreau is best known for the two years he spent living by Walden Pond in Massachusetts. This was an act of individualism, seeking a life of satisfaction and thinking. He believed that a person should work for only enough wages to be independent. Thus, he declined to go into his family's pencil business or become a teacher. Instead he earned what little money he needed by doing occasional surveying and odd jobs for Emerson. Although he lectured some, he was not widely known during his lifetime. His *Walden* (1854), observations of the world around him while living at the pond, is his best-known work. His essay "Civil Disobedience" is said to have provided inspiration to Gandhi. His championing of the individual against organized society and materialism led to widespread posthumous popularity of his writings.

The character of Washington has, after all, been undervalued, because not valued correctly. He was a proper Puritan hero. It is his erectness and persistency which attract me. A few simple deeds with a dignified silence for background, and that is all. He never fluctuated, nor lingered, nor stooped, nor swerved, but was nobly silent and assured. He was not the darling of the people, as no man of integrity can ever be, but was as much respected as loved. His instructions to his steward, his refusal of a Crown, his interview with his officers at the termination of the war, his thoughts of his retirement, as expressed in a letter to Lafayette, his remarks to another correspondent on his being chosen President, his last words to Congress, and the unparalleled respect which his most distinguished contemporaries, as Fox and Erskine, expressed for him, are refreshing to read in these unheroic days. His behavior in the field and in council, and his dignified and contented withdrawal to private life were great. He could advance and he could withdraw.

—From "Winter," December 25, 1840

HENRY DAVID THOREAU

ARTEMUS WARD

(CHARLES FARRAR BROWNE, 1834-67)

HUMORIST, JOURNALIST

For a pseudonym, Charles Farrar Browne borrowed the name of Artemus Ward, a Revolutionary War general who commanded the Massachusetts troops at Boston before Washington's arrival. As a young reporter on the *Cleveland Plain Dealer* in 1858, the latter-day Ward began a series of "Artemus Ward's Sayings," humorous columns which depended upon misspelling and rustic turns of phrase for their amusement value. His fame spread to both sides of the Atlantic with publication in 1862 of *Artemus Ward: His Book*. In 1859, he had joined the staff of *Vanity Fair,* then a humorous New York weekly. When the magazine failed, he immediately turned to lecturing, which proved popular and lucrative for the rest of his days.

G Washington was about the best man this country ever sot eyes on. He was a clear-headed, warm-hearted and stiddy goin man. He never slopt over! The prevailin' weakness of most public men is to SLOP OVER!...Washington never slopt over. That wasn't George's stile. He luved his country dearly. He wasn't after the spiles [spoils]. He was a human angil in a 3 kornered hat and knee britches.

—From "Fourth of July Oration," 1859

ARTEMUS WARD

DANIEL WEBSTER

(1782-1852)

ORATOR, STATESMAN, U.S. SENATOR, PRESIDENTIAL CANDIDATE

"The character of Washington...is a fixed star...."

The most renowned orator of his day, Daniel Webster was born in New Hampshire, graduated from Dartmouth College, and became a lawyer. Politics soon became his calling, and he served in the U.S. House of Representatives (1813-17 and 1823-27), then in the Senate (1827-41 and 1845-50). He was secretary of state in the William Henry Harrison–Zachary Taylor administration and again for President Millard Fillmore (1850-52).

Webster began his career as a Federalist and defender of New England shipping interests. He later supported, then broke with, President Andrew Jackson and became—with Henry Clay—a leader of the Whig party. Preservation of the

Union was of paramount concern to Webster, and his willingness to compromise in order to achieve this goal alienated the anti-slavery forces in the North and many of his own Whig supporters.

The character of Washington...is a fixed star in the firmament of great names, shining without twinkling or obscuration, with a clear, steady, beneficent light.

—Letter to the New York Committee for the Celebration of the Birthday of Washington, February 20, 1851

DANIEL WEBSTER

WALT WHITMAN
(1819-92)

POET

"...in defeat defeated not..."

In 1848, Walt Whitman traveled from New York to New Orleans, seeing the vastness of the American land for the first time. He set down his impressions in poems which became "Leaves of Grass." Within a context of celebrating democracy and nationhood, he wrote daringly about love, sex, pantheism, mysticism and his love of all humanity. Today, many critics consider him the greatest American poet.

The son of a Long Island carpenter, Whitman tried his hand at several occupations: printer, school teacher, reporter, newspaper editor. His early poems, from about 1841, were published in New York and Brooklyn newspapers. Whitman self-published the first edition of *Leaves of Grass* in 1855. He published expanded and revised editions throughout his life, the last one in 1892, the year he died. With its free verse and long rhythmic line, his approach to poetry was too radical for some. Ralph Waldo Emerson, however, praised *Leaves of Grass* in a congratulatory letter which Whitman included in the next edition.

During the Civil War, when he was a government clerk in Washington, D.C, he spent much time as a hospital volunteer, nursing wounded soldiers (including his brother). Many of his poems during his Washington years were inspired by a succession of male lovers. In addition to *Leaves of Grass,* his books of poems include *November Boughs, Calamus, Good-Bye My Fancy,* and *Sands at Seventy.* He also published several prose works.

The indomitable heart and arm—proofs of
  the never-broken line,
Courage, alertness, patience, faith, the same
  —e'en in defeat defeated not, the same.

—From "Washington's Monument, February 1985,"
in *November Boughs,* 1888

WALT WHITMAN

OSCAR WILDE
(1854-1900)

IRISH AUTHOR, PLAYWRIGHT, WIT

"...a man who was incapable of telling a lie."

Born in Dublin, schooled there and at Oxford, as a young writer Wilde soon drew the attention of the London literary establishment for his flamboyant "art-for-art's-sake" dress and his flouting of Victorian conventions. His sharp wit and satire brought him admirers and detractors. A collection of his poems was published in 1881, followed by a lecture tour of the United States in 1883 and a New York production of his play *Vera.* In 1884 he was married and began writing for a number of periodicals. A prolific and varied outpouring of fiction and plays followed. *The Picture of Dorian Gray,* a novel, and his drawing room comedies, *The Importance of Being Earnest* and *Lady Windemere's Fan,* are the best known. His London production of *Salome,* starring Sarah Bernhardt, was refused a license in 1893 but was, instead, performed in France. He was eventually tried and convicted for immoral conduct, and in 1895 was sent to prison, where he wrote his most famous work, *The Ballad of Reading Gaol.* He was released in 1897, and moved to France; he died in Paris.

The crude commercialism of America, its materialising spirit...are entirely due to the country having adopted for its national hero a man who was incapable of telling a lie.

—From "The Decay of Lying" (1889)

Washington's camp chest.

OSCAR WILDE

WOODROW WILSON

(1856-1924)

TWENTY-EIGHTH PRESIDENT OF THE UNITED STATES, 1912-21

*"Children desired sight of him,
and men felt lifted after he had passed."*

Son of a Presbyterian minister, Woodrow Wilson was born in Staunton, Virginia. After graduating from Princeton and obtaining a law degree at the University of Virginia, he practiced law briefly, then turned to academia, teaching history and political economy at Bryn Mawr and Wesleyan before becoming a professor at Princeton. He was elected president of that university in 1902. In 1910, he was elected governor of New Jersey; in 1912, he became president. Reelected in 1916 on the slogan "He kept us out of war," Wilson led the country into World War I the next year. Idealistic, he championed self-determination for all peoples. His health broke in 1919, and he failed to achieve his ambition to bring the United States into the League of Nations. Among the books he authored are *Congressional Government* (1885) and *George Washington* (1897).

There was something about Washington that quickened the pulses of a crowd at the same time it awed them, that drew cheers which were a sort of voice of worship. Children desired sight of him, and men felt lifted after he had passed. *

It was good to have such a man ride all the open way from Philadelphia to Cambridge, in sight of the people, to assume command of the people's army. It gave character to the thoughts of all who saw him.

—Description of Washington's trip to Massachusetts to take over the Continental Army, from *George Washington* (1897)

The real Washington was as thoroughly an American as Jackson or Lincoln. What we take for lack of passion in him was but the reserve and self-mastery natural to a man of his class and breeding in Virginia. He was no parlor politician, either. He had seen the frontier, and far beyond it where the French forts lay. He knew the rough life of the country as few other men could. His thoughts did not live at Mount Vernon. He knew difficulty as intimately and faced it always with as quiet a mastery as William the Silent.

—From *Mere Literature* (1896)

* This paragraph is noted in pencil in the flyleaf of Wilson's widow's personal copy of the book as a "description of G.W. which so perfectly describes Woodrow Wilson himself."

WOODROW WILSON

PART III

WASHINGTON TODAY—AND TOMORROW

DAVID ABSHIRE

AMBASSADOR, PRESIDENTIAL COUNSELOR, HISTORIAN, PUBLIC-POLICY RESEARCH INSTITUTE CO-FOUNDER

Ambassador, presidential counselor, historian, public-policy research institute co-founder

"To Washington, slaves were also people."

A 1951 graduate of the United States Military Academy at West Point, David Abshire received his doctoral degree in history from Georgetown University, where he was an adjunct professor for twelve years at its School of Foreign Service. He has served as assistant secretary of state for congressional relations, U.S. ambassador to NATO, and special counsel to President Reagan (1987). In 1962, he co-founded the Center for Strategic and International Studies (CSIS), a public-policy research institute in Washington, D.C., where he is now vice chairman of the board of trustees. He is also president and chief executive officer of the Center for the Study of the Presidency. He is the author of five books.

To Washington, slaves were also people. He treated his slaves with benevolence. He decided that he wished to free his slaves and see to the care of the old and infirm among them, but was vexed by the problem of how to live without them at his beloved Mount Vernon. Unable to find a solution practical to the context of 18th-century Virginia, he decided to set his slaves free upon his wife's death. Their liberation might seem to some like a "deathbed conversion." That is, too little, too late. Yet, while the bitter experience of slavery in America would persist for many years to come, this act stands as a remarkable sort of conscientious objection for the times. Though sentimentally attached to his way of life, through his travels and experiences he arrived at the prescient conclusion that, according to a friend, "I can clearly foresee that nothing but the rooting out of slavery can perpetuate the existence of our union."

DAVID ABSHIRE

LAMAR ALEXANDER

GOVERNOR, U.S. SECRETARY OF EDUCATION, PRESIDENTIAL CANDIDATE

"In office, he created a balance of familiarity and restraint...."

A seventh-generation Tennessean, Lamar Alexander served as governor of his state from 1979-87. Upon leaving office he co-founded a company (now publicly traded) that provides on-site child-care facilities for corporations. Later in 1987 he was named president of the University of Tennessee and served through 1990, when then-President George Bush appointed him U.S. secretary of education, a post he held through the rest of the Bush term. Over the course of his career he has authored seven books. In 1996 and in 1999 he was a candidate for the Republican nomination for President of the United States.

Approaching Mount Rushmore Memorial in the Black Hills of South Dakota you first see George Washington—sixty feet high from chin to hairline—imagining, it seems to me, that there could be a country such as ours; then Jefferson, imagining what that country could become; then Lincoln imagining that it was worth saving. In between Jefferson and Lincoln is Teddy Roosevelt, imagining that we could do anything we set our minds to.

These four presidents dreamed big and then brought out the best in this nation to make those dreams realities. They showed us what can happen when we set our standards high.

George Washington set his standards especially high. He named the new chief executive "Mr. President," and fashioned a new form of unifying leadership that would serve as a democratic substitute for the royal family, aristocratic traditions and the national Church of England. Our first president delivered the first State of the Union address, hired the first (five-person) presidential staff, and took the first presidential tour to feel the pulse of the people. In office, he created a balance of familiarity and restraint that, for the most part, continued until recently. He declined to make his vice-president prime minister, thereby leaving the executive's ceremonial and governing functions all wrapped up within the single office of president. He startled a world filled with monarchs by voluntarily relinquishing his office after two terms. This especially confounded

LAMAR ALEXANDER

Napoleon who had said, "Whenever I see a throne, I have the urge to sit on it."

Washington's deeds and his character were inseparable. He may have been our most charismatic president, with a certain dignity, towering physical presence and studied sense of theater. He was an expert dancer and Virginia's best horseman. But his charisma was not like the swagger of a Roosevelt or a Kennedy. He was not especially eloquent. He did not dazzle with his legislative skills. His was a "charisma of competence," based upon what he actually did, and his sincere commitment to his country.

At a time when the American presidency has been dragged through the gutter, it is useful to be reminded how grand the presidency can be— when properly occupied. George Washington's relevance today is this: He reminds us that an American president must accept the responsibility of serving as the national role model. The president's job is selecting urgent needs, developing strategies, and persuading at least half the people that he is right. But the job requires more than that. It requires understanding that the American president's character is an essential part of our national character. Washington knew it instinctively.

LETITIA BALDRIGE

AUTHORITY ON MANNERS, ETIQUETTE, PROTOCOL; MANAGEMENT-TRAINING CONSULTANT

"He was the exact opposite of 'political correctness.'"

From the beginning, Letitia Baldrige's career prepared her to become America's leading authority on manners. Her first position was as social secretary to the U.S. ambassador in Paris. Next was a stint as an intelligence officer in the State Department in Washington, D.C., followed by three years as assistant to the U.S. ambassador in Rome. She left government service to become public relations director for Tiffany & Co., then was social secretary in the Kennedy White House. Since 1964, she has headed her own firm, specializing in training management executives in interaction with colleagues. She is the author of sixteen books, most recently *More Than Manners! Raising Today's Kids to Have Kind Manners and Good Hearts* (1997). She has served on the advisory boards of the Woodrow Wilson House, Washington, D.C., and George Washington's home and estate, Mount Vernon, Virginia.

When George Washington was about fifteen, his schoolmaster gave him as a class exercise the copying of a sixteenth-century book of rules of civility by a Jesuit priest. Young George did more than copy the rules. He modernized them to fit his own times. The result was "Rules of Civility and Good Behavior." There are one hundred and nine in all. He covered many things that are apt today, such as "Think before you speak. Pronounce not imperfectly nor bring out your words too hastily." Now that is a rule of manners, but also of kindness, because it means that when you follow it, people can understand what you say without asking you to repeat yourself. A corollary was his, "Interrupt him not, nor answer him until his speech be ended."

Washington treated everyone with respect unless there was a reason not to do so. His first rule of civility was that everything done in company should be done with courtesy toward those present. One of the things I like best about Washington is his kindness toward others. In the book, he interspersed stern dictums with kindly advice.

"Rules of Civility" tells us quite a lot about the forces that shaped George Washington's character. He had to grow up early. His mother was widowed, and he helped with his siblings. His work on the "Rules" book shows that he was worried that his contemporaries didn't know enough about how to behave. Even at that early age he seemed to understand instinctively that a lack of manners contributes to chaos in society; to doing things sloppily and less well. He became a perfectionist, demanding the highest standards, first of himself.

He was an awkward teenager, very tall and with acne, yet he grew to become a handsome man among mostly short people. He was commanding in stature. This almost certainly contributed to his leadership. Tall people were rare in those days.

He respected others and expected it in return. This respect and courtesy toward others was bonded inside him; it could not be turned on and off like a faucet. He did not just summon it to impress others. As a result, he had the intense loyalty of his officers and men. They really adored him. But so did his field hands and slaves. He would have considered it a terrible thing to let any of them down through bad behavior, such as loose temper, abusive language or drunkenness.

He had great deference for protocol, but he was not a martinet. He was the exact opposite of what today would be called "political correctness." In his day, the standard of the age was to pay homage to the leader. While he applied his "rules of civility" to men and women, in their wording he doesn't really let the ladies in. While that is bothersome today, it, too, was the standard of the age.

LETITIA BALDRIGE

I do not think of George Washington as being a particularly religious man, at least not in the church-going sense. God, however, was present in his daily life. Everyone in Washington's time was more conscious of God's role in everyday life than is the case today, and he was no exception. Indeed, one of his rules of civility is "Labor to keep alive in your breast a celestial fire."

Washington's address card.

PATRICK J. BUCHANAN

PRESIDENTIAL CANDIDATE, COMMUNICATIONS DIRECTOR AT THE WHITE HOUSE, AUTHOR, COLUMNIST, COMMENTATOR

"Foreign policy was...among the causes that brought Washington to Philadelphia."

A native of the nation's capital, Pat Buchanan holds a master's degree from Columbia University. His journalistic career began as an editorial writer at the *St. Louis Globe-Democrat.* From 1968-74, he served as a special assistant to President Richard Nixon. On leaving the White House he became a syndicated newspaper columnist and commentator on major television programs. From 1985-87 he served as White House director of communications for President Ronald Reagan. He participated in four summits—two of Nixon's and two of Reagan's. In 1992, he challenged President Bush for the Republican nomination. In 1996, he contested for the nomination again, winning the New Hampshire primary and finishing second to Senator Robert

Dole. He again declared his candidacy for the presidency in
the 2000 campaign. The most recent of his four books is *A
Republic, Not an Empire.*

When Washington returned to Mount Vernon
after Yorktown, he was no longer simply a
Virginian. The war had seared into his soul the first
principle of the foreign policy he would shape for
his country: Sever all political and military ties to
Europe. Four times in a century, Americans had
gone to war because the Mother Country had.
Never again. No cause on the blood-soaked continent was worth the life of a single American.

Washington had welcomed the 1778 Treaty of Alliance
with France. It must, he said, "chalk out a plain and
easy road to independence." That alliance had brought
Admiral DeGrasse's fleet and Rochambeau's army to
Yorktown. But with victory, Americans began to look
for ways to sever the alliance.

To Washington, alliances were to be temporary,
entered into when a crisis commanded, dissolved
when the crisis passed. Just before he took office as
president, Washington wrote Lafayette:

"While you are quarreling among yourselves in
Europe, while one King is running mad and others
acting as if they were already so by cutting the
throats of the subjects of their neighbours, I think
you need not doubt, my dear Marquis, we shall
continue in tranquility here."

Washington also differed from his great contemporaries in that he was a man of the West. From his experiences in the French and Indian War and earlier as a surveyor in the wilderness, he saw America's future in the West.

But as he looked west, Washington saw America's natural expansion blocked. Farmers and frontiersmen, unable to ship bulk goods over the mountains, had to move them by water. Spain, however, controlled the Mississippi, outlet to the sea for the citizens of Kentucky, Tennessee, western Virginia and western Pennsylvania, and had closed New Orleans to American commerce.

West of Georgia and south of the Tennessee, Creek, Choctaw and Cherokee had been taken under Spanish protection and were being armed. Spain thus held the keys to peace, prosperity and security in the Southwest.

In the Northwest, the outlook was equally grim. Britain controlled the Great Lakes and the St. Lawrence and had refused to honor that part of the peace treaty which dictated surrender of the forts that controlled access to the sea. Britain was using what it held illegally to block America's trade.

With his country recovering from its Revolution, Washington did not want another war. Rather than confront Spain or Britain, he opted for the "arts of peace," clearing rivers, building bridges and establishing conveniences for traveling to tie the West to the Atlantic with bonds of commerce…. If the

PATRICK J. BUCHANAN

seaboard could establish trade ties with the western-
ers, before Spain and Britain could lure them away,
the West would be America's forever.

Foreign policy was thus inseparable from domestic
policy and was high among the causes that brought
Washington to Philadelphia. He feared a British-
Spanish strategy of encirclement, containment and
strangulation was designed to abort a united
America to the Mississippi, and he had come to
believe that only a strong central government could
deal with the crowing and bullying. Washington
also wanted a new constitution to outlaw state
tariffs and end internal trade wars, so the confederation could be tied together with bonds of commerce, and America could gradually reduce its
dependence upon Europe, especially Great Britain.

The constitution created that executive, and, in
Washington, America had the indispensable man to
steer it through the most perilous years of its existence. From 1789 to 1797, the policies of
Washington effected the de facto annexation of the
Northwest Territory that America had possessed
only de jure before he became president. Equally
critical, our first president had kept his vulnerable
country out of the wars exploding across Europe.

—From *A Republic, Not an Empire*
(Regnery Publishing, Inc.)

ROBERT DOLE

PRESIDENTIAL CANDIDATE, U.S. SENATE MAJORITY LEADER

*"The United States itself is
Washington's greatest accomplishment."*

Born and reared in Russell, on the plains of western Kansas, Robert Dole led the U.S. Senate in 1985-86 and 1994-96, capping seventeen years in that body, after six in the House of Representatives. He also served as Republican national chairman from 1970-72. In 1996 he was the Republican nominee for president. Of Bob Dole as Senate majority leader, Ronald Reagan said, "His title of Leader is not just a job title; it's a description of the man." Seriously wounded in the Italian campaign in World War II, Bob Dole was determined to rebound from a slow and painful recovery—and did—to take up a career in law and later politics. His honors include the Purple Heart and Bronze Star with two clusters for his war service, and the Presidential Medal of Freedom.

ROBERT DOLE

Being from Kansas, I have a weakness for anyone who can administer a farm as well as George Washington did. In his case, of course, it was a series of farms, totaling thirteen square miles, with more workers than Washington oversaw in the Executive branch of the new national government.

Farmers are practical people, both patient and innovative. Washington's ability to evolve new farm techniques, his shift from tobacco to wheat and other crops, his entrepreneurial outlook and basic self-sufficiency, were all emblematic of an outlook that enabled him to lead an uphill struggle against a superior military force, and an economically underdeveloped nation whose interests were precariously balanced between manufacturing and agriculture.

Modern politicians would do the country a service by cultivating Washington-style civility. Alas, in some quarters these days, civility is confused with weakness, and compromise—the essence of the American constitutional experiment over which Washington would preside—with surrender. In fact, Washington spent a lifetime earning the respect of his countrymen. He was no less determined to respect them, including those with whom he might disagree. The wheels of government might grind more slowly in a democratic nation, he once observed, "But the people, at last, will be right." No one understood better than he that in a democratic system trust is the coin of the realm. No leader who fails to trust the people can expect to win or keep their trust.

I think Washington's greatest success was to disprove the conventional view that so-called common people were incapable of self-government. In the Revolution he had refuted Old World expectations that colonials could not stand up to the world's greatest empire. Later, as president, Washington almost single-handedly insured the success of the first republic in nearly two jthousand years. He did so, not by issuing orders or assuming dictatorial powers, but by preaching restraint, balancing opposing factions and foregoing U.S. involvement in Europe's murderous wars. The United States itself is Washington's greatest achievement.

In the Revolution, Washington risked everything in the service of his country. As president, he risked his hard-won reputation and peace of mind. Through it all, he subordinated his private interests to the public good. And, while he took strenuous objection to the press and to political criticism directed his way, he did so in private. Never did he give vent to his anger in public. Pure character.

ROBERT DOLE

ALVIN S. FELZENBERG
WRITER AND LECTURER ABOUT THE PRESIDENCY

"...Washington all but vanished from a holiday that Revolutionary War soldiers began celebrating in 1777."

Although his vocation is government service, Al Felzenberg's passion is the presidency of the United States. He is the author of numerous articles on the subject and was co-editor of *Evolution of the Modern Presidency: A Bibliographical Survey,* published by the American Enterprise Institute. He earned bachelor's and master's degrees at Rutgers University, then a master's and Ph.D. in politics from Princeton. He has been a lecturer in politics at Princeton, assistant secretary of state of New Jersey, senior deputy chairman of the National Endowment for the Arts, and executive director of the President's Commission on Appointments. Since 1997 he has been staff director of the Empowerment Subcommittee of the Small Business Committee of the U.S House of Representatives.

Holidays are a nation's way of signaling what it considers important. July 4 is such a day. February 22 once was, too.

That changed in 1968 when Congress passed the Monday Holiday Law. Although its legal name remained "Washington's Birthday," businesses, the news media and calendars took to calling the February holiday "Presidents' Day." In 1971, President Richard Nixon issued a proclamation urging Americans to honor—on the third Monday of February—all who had served as president.

Years passed and George Washington all but vanished from a holiday that Revolutionary War soldiers began celebrating in 1777. When Congress declared Washington's birthday a national holiday late in the last century, it was following widespread community practices.

Washington's diminished standing in the "hearts of his countrymen" today is partially the by-product of the "political correctness" of the age. It may also signify the nation's admission that it is no longer sure what values it wishes to enshrine.

Just as "Presidents' Day" was taking hold, academicians who demanded that history be taught "from the bottom up" began winning out. Some said their goal was to include in the American story people and groups who had been "left out."

ALVIN S. FELZENBERG

"Greats" gave way to the ordinary. Washington, a "dead white male," who was both a general and a president, was ripe for the picking.

Others had a broader agenda. Under the banner of "cultural relativism," they tore into traditional national symbols. The New Orleans School Board unanimously voted to remove Washington's name from a school because he owned slaves. One activist proclaimed that Washington had as much meaning to African-Americans as David Duke. Really?

Washington became just one of the forty-two men who had been president. His contributions were no more stressed and praised than those of Franklin Pierce.

Once "leveled" Washington was "humanized." One book claimed Washington had "padded" his expense account. Others accused him of unsavory "land speculations."

In the age of Dr. Ruth, comedians joked about all the places Washington had slept. There were wisecracks about his "wooden teeth."

News that the cherry tree story and others were fiction was taken as proof that Washington's integrity may have been less pure than his earlier biographers said. Those drawing that conclusion forgot that myths are based on fact, intended as parables.

Abraham Lincoln remembered. En route to his inauguration in 1861, Lincoln told the New Jersey State Senate how inspired he had been when he read Parson Weems's "Life of Washington" at the age of fourteen:

"I recollect thinking then, boy even though I was, that there must have been something more than common that those men struggled for...that something even more than national independence; that something that held out a great promise to all the people of the world for all time to come."

In 1932, the commission that oversaw the Washington birth bicentennial used Washington's example to entice Americans to become part of something bigger than themselves. They began the all-but-now-defunct practice of Washington's Birthday pageants, plays, parades and essay contests, and placed reproductions of Gilbert Stuart's portrait of Washington in thousands of classrooms.

The turn of another century is an opportunity for the nation to recommit itself to the values that gave it life and stir the world still. It can begin by bringing "Washington's Birthday" back into the American lexicon. George Washington can still be of service to his country.

ALVIN S. FELZENBERG

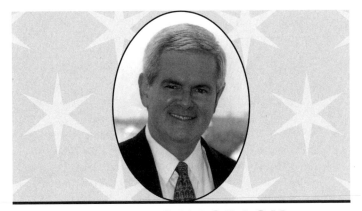

NEWT GINGRICH

SPEAKER OF THE U.S. HOUSE OF REPRESENTATIVES, 1995-98

"He was a remarkable manager of personalities."

Elected to Congress in 1978, Newt Gingrich led the Republicans to a House majority in the election of 1994, for the first time since 1952. He became the first Republican Speaker of the House since 1928 to be re-elected to that leadership post. He is acknowledged as the chief architect of his party's "Contract with America." In 1995, *Time* magazine named him Man of the Year. Before being elected to Congress, he taught history and environmental studies at West Georgia College. He is the author of several books. He chose not to stand a third time for election as speaker, and resigned his seat in the House in early 1999. Today he is in private business in Georgia.

There are two important things for our generation to understand about George Washington.

First, that America would not have developed into the country it has become if Washington had not been the dominant founding father. Our nation and culture are permanently imprinted by his attitudes, characteristics and policies. Many of the foundations upon which our present-day opinions and philosophical tenets rest can be traced directly to this most reserved yet indispensable man.

The second important fact for our generation is that Washington is distinct from modern figures. It is virtually impossible to understand him in a contemporary American setting; to truly understand things he valued. Washington was a man who deliberately kept himself aloof. He firmly believed that character mattered. He also believed that gentlemen had conscious limitations on their behavior. He felt others would rally to the symbol of his being. *Who* he was mattered more than *what* he said.

Today, in an age of shameless talk shows and shallow politicians, George Washington seems almost inexplicable. Yet, like Charles de Gaulle of France in a later period, he understood that to personify a nation was vastly more important than talking about one. He understood the symbols of patriotism, honesty, courage and endurance, and to live those words was immensely more important than describing them. Washington was, in that sense, Roman rather than Greek. He lacked the oratorical

NEWT GINGRICH

ability of a Pericles or a Demosthenes, but he precisely resembled Cincinnatus and Horatius in living the patriotism and dedication that are essential to national leadership.

As this country was being founded, what mattered most to the American people was that they had as their leader a serious, patriotic and disciplined authority figure who understood that to be the father of one's country, one had to behave like a father. He was a man with a deep sense of history, respect for the rule of law, and an understanding of both the potentiality and limitations of ordinary human beings.

Washington especially excelled in this last sense. He was a remarkable manager of personalities, as he proved by keeping such strong rivals as Alexander Hamilton and Thomas Jefferson in double harness in his cabinet. He had an equal, quiet ability to inspire average citizens, as shown by his capacity to keep an exhausted and half-starved army at Valley Forge. Finally, he held the respect of men of better education and far greater literary talent—all of whom organized themselves around his leadership and sought to influence his decisions. In the end, such men regarded Washington as morally superior and as a man of far greater authority than they. In the eulogies after his death, virtually every leading contemporary admitted that Washington was truly the indispensable man.

There are three things that illuminate Washington's career. First, that he relished Addison's play, *Cato,* and saw in Roman republican symbols the ultimate virtues that would last in history, including the willingness of Cato to die rather than serve a tyrant. Washington valued these republican virtues above popularity or the more traditional forms of power.

Secondly, he was willing to give up power when he could have been the dictator or monarch of the new country. When his own rebellious officer corps asked him to take over the Continental Congress, Washington proclaimed that he had hardly rebelled against George III in order to become George I!

The third of Washington's great strengths was his patient endurance; endurance that avoided defeat rather than the brilliance which insured victory. He had patience that few leaders have matched. He was willing to calmly establish right principles while avoiding wrong actions, all the time he was in the field (three years during the French and Indian War, eight years during the Revolutionary War), in semi-retirement for five years, then finally as president for eight years. In sum, Washington understood that the right minimum of accomplishments with few mistakes is vastly more powerful than a more glorious set of achievements marred by large mistakes.

Almost none of the personal characteristics of George Washington fit the modern age's sense of immediate dialogue, self-revelation, achievement and instant gratification. This mismatch—this lack of his characteristics in our leaders, culture, society and citizens—is to our discredit rather than to Washington's diminishment.

NEWT GINGRICH

CAREW LEE
REGENT, MOUNT VERNON LADIES' ASSOCIATION

"...a man...for all our centuries."

Carew Lee (Mrs. Robert E. Lee IV) serves as chairperson ("Regent") of the thirty-one-member, all-woman board that governs Mount Vernon, George Washington's estate on the Potomac River. She was elected to a three-year term, 1997-99, representing Maryland on the board since 1972. Prior to serving as regent for the Mount Vernon Ladies' Association, which owns and operates Mount Vernon, she served as chairperson of its development committee and as president of the Mount Vernon Inn restaurant and retail complex. In addition to chairing two full board meetings every year, she presides over twenty-two standing committees and serves as Mount Vernon's official hostess. In 1999, under her leadership, Mount Vernon mounted three traveling exhibits and an unprecedented array of on-site programs and special events to commemorate the two hundredth anniversary of Washington's death.

We are about to begin the twenty-first century and people ask me what can we learn from a man who died at the end of the eighteenth century? My short answer is, "Plenty." Two qualities in particular, however, stand out as being urgently needed today. One is high standards. George Washington set tall ones for himself and led by example. The other is determination. He was determined to win the war despite heavy odds against him.

Our interest in self-sacrifice, hard work, self-discipline, honesty and integrity all seem to be slipping away today. All of these were things George Washington considered essential to a successful nation. He expected them to be taught in the family and in the schools. He believed that a good country required good citizens who maintained standards for themselves.

As president, Washington felt that he had to keep high standards so that others would look to him and realize how important it was for them to keep their own standards high. He made mistakes, of course, but he always learned from them.

As for determination, I believe the Revolutionary War would never have been won without his determination to succeed. He never gave up, no matter how grim the situation. He had a Congress that didn't feed his soldiers. I think it is amazing that he kept his troops' morale high and kept them together. The sojourn at Morristown

CAREW LEE

really pointed it out. Almost no food, no tents, little ammunition, many diseases and no doctors. But they stayed together because of one man, Washington.

He was a man not just for the eighteenth century, but for all our centuries.

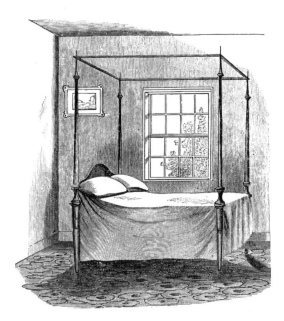

Bed and bedstead on which Washington died.

EUGENE McCARTHY

AUTHOR, U.S. SENATOR,
PRESIDENTIAL CANDIDATE

*"He was concerned that strong political parties
would be divisive."*

Eugene McCarthy represented Minnesota in the U.S. Senate from 1959-70. Before that he was a member of the House of Representatives (1946-59), but he is best known for his anti–Vietnam War candidacy for the Democratic presidential nomination in 1968. Supported by legions of enthusiastic young campaign workers, he had such a strong showing in the New Hampshire primary that President Lyndon Johnson soon announced he would not stand for reelection. He is the author of many books, including *No Fault Politics*.

Washington's important contribution to the country was that he held it together. Both the Adams faction and the Jeffersonians turned to him. I think it was a combination of respect for him and recollection of what he did in the war.

If he had not been willing to serve, there would have been a split, perhaps not irreparable, but nevertheless a serious problem. We don't realize just how tenuous that government was under the Articles of Confederation—before the Constitution. There were a great many concessions to the individual states. For example, senators were treated as if they were ambassadors. There were real threats of states breaking away. With the Constitution ratified, Washington, by limiting himself to two terms, set a personal example for all others to follow. After all, there were some around him who favored the restoration of imperial trappings. He was opposed to that, as he was opposed to partisan politics.

He was concerned that strong political parties would be divisive. He worried about one political party. He didn't want any. As for two parties, he was concerned not so much about one party dominating the scene as he was that the friction between two parties would create issues peripheral to the problems of the country. When you have two parties that don't have significant differences you get what we have today: attacks on personalities. Washington wanted to be, and was, a unifying figure. Everyone had great respect for him. After he left the scene, the party system was inevitable and developed over the next twenty to thirty years.

DAVID McCULLOUGH

HISTORIAN

"He had such tremendous courage, nerve, and a willingness to take risks...."

Twice winner of the National Book Award and the Francis Parkman Prize and a Pulitzer Prize winner, David McCullough is widely known for his narrative history books: *The Johnstown Flood, The Great Bridge, The Path Between the Seas, Mornings on Horseback, Brave Companions,* and *Truman.* To television audiences he is known as the host of public television's "The American Experience," and as the narrator of many documentaries, including "The Civil War." A citation accompanying an honorary degree awarded him by his alma mater, Yale University, reads, "As an historian, he paints with words, giving us pictures of the American people that live, breathe, and above all, confront the fundamental issues of courage, achievement and moral character."

DAVID McCULLOUGH

The old familiar scenes, the cliches about Washington, actually do capture the essence of the man. Even Parson Weems's little story about the cherry tree, silly as it may be, conveys the fundamental truth of his honesty. Or, consider "Washington Crossing the Delaware." That's one of the greatest moments in American history—and very revealing. He had such tremendous courage, nerve, and a willingness to take risks, and he was emboldened not just by his own bravery and audacity, but by total devotion to the cause of America.

There he was, down to just a few thousand half-starved troops, having retreated ignominiously across New Jersey, with no support from the local populace. The best army in the world was bearing down on him. His only recourse was to cross the river and put it between him and the British, then presumably lick his wounds on the other side.

But what does he do? He attacks! Imagine, he crosses back over the river again in driving sleet and snow and attacks, hits the enemy after they've gone into winter quarters at Trenton—and on Christmas night!

Jefferson said Washington's most important characteristic was prudence. He must have been thinking of Washington as president, because as commander of the Continental Army some of his most effective actions were notably imprudent. Surprise was the essence.

Think what he'd done at Boston when he put the guns on Dorchester Heights. It was audacious in the extreme, almost unimaginable, and all accomplished, in secret, in a single night. One of the British officers said, "My God, these fellows have more work in one night than I could make my army do in three months."

Compared with the British commanders he was facing, Washington had had hardly any experience. He'd been out of the army for some seventeen years, and had never commanded anything as large as a regiment. He'd had no experience with artillery. But none of that stopped him.

One of his greatest qualities was that he wouldn't give up. He grew in the job and the army grew in its job with him. And that, of course, is very American. They learned by doing it.

Washington just stubbornly refused to succumb to the onerous reality that the odds were so heavily against him. He did a lot of complaining— indeed, whining—to Congress, and especially about its failure to pay his men. But in that, his humanity comes through. He wasn't the marble man so often depicted.

I find his love of fox hunting, dancing, cards, and the theater all very appealing. His terrible temper—which he learned to control—is also clearly very human. Nor should his entrepreneurial impulses—the canal projects, the land speculation—be seen as incongruous.

DAVID MCCULLOUGH

He was an active, energetic man of his time, a strong man. When he came into a room, people knew someone important had arrived. Abigail Adams, as astute a judge of people as anyone of that day, thought her husband's praise for the general a bit restrained, given her impressions. Washington was six-foot-four in his boots—quite unusual then—and knew full well the importance of how he appeared.

I think the people who hold up the longest in the nation's memory are those who best personify— legitimately personify—great events. In his own time, Washington personified, as did no one else, both the success of the revolution and the establishment of a new nation. It's no wonder he was idolized. The fact that he was the intrepid leader through thick and thin—and remember, it was mostly thin—and triumphed, made him irresistibly important and appealing. Right from the start as president, he set very high standards for the office; and dignity was among the most important of those standards. He created the presidential ideal, an American ideal, and of this, too, he was quite conscious.

It's not fashionable now to praise great men or women. It's argued that this or that figure from the past wasn't great because he or she wasn't perfect. Greatness and perfection, however, are not synonymous. Of course there have been great Americans, many of them, and George Washington was one of the very greatest.

GEORGE McGOVERN

PRESIDENTIAL CANDIDATE,
UNITED STATES SENATOR (1963-81)

"Character has always seemed to me to be the defining greatness of George Washington."

The study of history and the production of food have been major interests of George McGovern throughout his career. He was a professor of history at Dakota Wesleyan University in South Dakota when he ran for and was elected to the U.S. House of Representatives in 1956. He served two terms. In 1961, President Kennedy appointed him as the first director of the U.S. Food for Peace program. In 1962, he was elected to the U.S. Senate and was re-elected in 1968 and 1974. In 1972, he was the Democratic Party's nominee for President of the United States. Later, Presidents Ford and Carter appointed him as a delegate to the United Nations. He has been a visiting professor at a number of leading universities. He is the author of seven books. In March 1998, he became U.S. ambassador to the U.N. Food and Agricultural Agencies in Rome.

George Washington did not have the originality of mind of Madison, Jefferson or Hamilton, but he had other great strengths that have rightfully given him a crucial, central role in the early years of our nation.

His leadership during the revolution was a major factor in the success of that effort. The confidence that he enjoyed of his fellow Americans and his soldiers—from the beginning—was indispensable to the success of the Revolutionary War.

When considering his presidency, one is hard-pressed to think of any other of the early figures in our history who could have successfully kept, in the same Cabinet, such men as Thomas Jefferson and Alexander Hamilton. He saw the strengths in both men, and he was able to draw appreciably from both.

The genius of American politics has always involved the creative tension between liberalism and conservatism. Those two traditions have served America well from the beginning. Our greatest presidents have drawn from the insights and the strengths of both conservatism and liberalism. The American political system has worked best when both of these traditions were clearly defined and actively defended.

It is the great political genius of Washington that he understood the necessity of unifying the nation while permitting vigorous debate to occur between these two major competing traditions, as well as various secondary political points of view, and to find a ruling consensus around which the country could be governed.

It may be an overworked word, but "character" has always seemed to me to be the defining greatness of George Washington.

Washington's Lepine watch, seal, and key.

GEORGE MCGOVERN

RONALD REAGAN

Fortieth President of the United States, 1981-89

"He personified a people...."

Climaxing a series of careers—radio broadcasting, films, television, a labor union presidency, Governor of California—Ronald Reagan was inaugurated president in January 1981, with three priorities: fix an ailing economy and set it on course of long-term growth, curb the growth of the federal government, and bring the Cold War to an end. He accomplished the first, began the process for the second, and pursued a series of policy measures that brought Mikhail Gorbachev to the point where he had no alternative but to give up the Cold War. Not long afterward, the Soviet Union, itself, ceased to exist. Throughout his long and successful public career, Reagan drew inspiration from the Founding Fathers of the nation, especially Washington. He shared a number of Washington's qualities: setting clear goals, personal modesty, respect for others, the ability to inspire those around him, and, above all, determination.

The image of George Washington kneeling in prayer in the snow is one of the most famous in American history. He personified a people who knew it was not enough to depend on their own courage and goodness; they must also seek help from God, their Father and Preserver.

Christmas radio address to the nation, December 24, 1983

RONALD REAGAN

RICHARD NORTON SMITH

PRESIDENTIAL BIOGRAPHER

"Two hundred years after his death, our first president remains universally recognized—and virtually unknown."

Richard Norton Smith has combined careers as a biographer, historian, and Washington speechwriter with that of an innovative director of presidential libraries and museums. His books include *Patriarch: George Washington and the New American Nation, An Uncommon Man: The Triumph of Herbert Hoover, Thomas E. Dewey and His Times, The Colonel: The Life and Legend of Robert R. McCormick,* and a "biography" of his alma mater, *The Harvard Century: The Making of a University and a Nation.* He has served as director of the Herbert Hoover Presidential Library and Museum, the Dwight D. Eisenhower Center, the Ronald Reagan Presidential Library, and currently is director of the Gerald R. Ford Museum and Library.

Two hundred years after his death, our first president remains universally recognized—and virtually unknown. For example, while most Americans think of him as a born aristocrat, he was in fact the eldest son of a second marriage, whose prospects were far from encouraging. Beyond the accident of birth, Washington's entire life would be a struggle, first to establish a sense of self-independence of his vinegary mother, and then to subdue his volatile emotions.

Young Washington never stopped learning or putting his new-found knowledge to practical use. At an early age he could ford a river, clothe a regiment, chart a mountain road and charm a lawmaker. While still a teenager, he pocketed five hundred acres of Virginia's Frederick County as a surveyor's fee. Over the next few years his land holdings tripled, providing a ticket of admission to the colonial gentry, whose esteem he valued at least as much as their hospitable company.

What was it about Washington that led his colleagues to choose him to lead the Continental Army? The simplest answer is one word: character. That, and the unglamorous, undramatic strengths: perseverance, fidelity to a cause larger than oneself, an almost superhuman capacity for sustained work, strategic and political skills greater than those of his contemporaries. Washington was willing to sacrifice not just his fortune but his future and his reputation—the latter of far greater value to him—in the pursuit of American independence.

RICHARD NORTON SMITH

Later, as president, he surrendered his declining years—a period when he seems almost most human because he was most vulnerable—in the hope that the American experiment might disprove doubters who questioned man's capacity for self-government. For this he paid an enormous cost in peace of mind, seeing his motives and even his honesty shredded by newspapers filled with scurrilous attacks. In the process, he demonstrated that it was possible to love one's country more than oneself—a timeless lesson, applicable in every generation.

To his everlasting credit, George Washington was ambiguous about power. The man who could have been king insisted that ultimate sovereignty lay with the people, however imperfect their judgment. At the end of the war, and again at the end of his presidency, he calmly walked away from power. This genius for renunciation prompted the dying Napoleon in his windswept exile to remark, "They wanted me to be another Washington." But of course that was impossible. Two hundred years later, our first president remains that rarest of historical figures of whom it can be said that, in conceding his humanity, we only confirm his greatness.

R. EMMETT TYRRELL, JR.

WRITER, EDITOR

"...he recognized the nation's democratic essence."

Bob Tyrrell is founder and editor-in-chief of the *American Spectator*, a political and cultural monthly magazine (and daily website). He is also a syndicated columnist, a frequent guest on television public affairs programs, and the author of several books, including *Boy Clinton, The Impeachment of William Jefferson Clinton, The Conservative Crack-up, The Liberal Crack-up*, and *Public Nuisances*.

It is fitting that the capital of the United States should be named "Washington," after the republic's first great military leader and president, George Washington. Incidentally, he was a fine military leader, and one of his first exploits while serving as a lieutenant colonel in the Virginia militia was a victory with vast consequences. Leading a small band of Virginians and Indians, he fell upon a detachment of French soldiers at a remote corner of the wilderness, the future site of Pittsburgh. Here was Washington, a nobody fighting in the swales of nowhere, but this paltry altercation set off a world war, the Seven Years War, fought in North America, the Caribbean, Central and South America, the Atlantic, India and Europe. Thus, the first president of the country destined to end the world's most destructive world wars actually ignited the first world war.

The eponym for Washington, D.C., had a more proximate influence on the country he helped to found. As a general and as a political leader he set the direction of the young republic—in terms of governance and disposition—for years to come; and remember, the disposition of a nation is as important to its well-being as the disposition of an individual.

The disposition of the revolutionary period had been daring, occasionally to the point of foolhardiness. The firebrands of the revolutionary movement were fine for stirring things up, but once independence was at hand it was time to settle things down. Yet, among some of the erstwhile colonists, bloody-mindedness was still fevering their brows. They did not want to pay their debts or adapt to a central government, and they were fetched by the bloody delusions of the French radicals. Fortunately, the old soldier who had led the revolutionary army and now served as president did not share this disposition. His was more sober. To be sure, he had been willing to gamble his considerable fortune for independence from the king. But his behavior in politics was sober, deliberate, prudent and restrained.

The consequence was that our bankrupt, war-worn and anarchic young country was not snookered into European wars as radicals at home and abroad wanted. Nor did the new president—either through imperiousness or timidity—allow the thirteen colonies to slip further into anarchy. Washington judiciously developed the American presidency and its foreign policy. Without his steady restraint things could have gone very badly. During his first administration Washington recognized that if he fully utilized the latent powers that the Constitution seemed to grant the president, he could have been perceived as a tyrant. He had a veto over congressional legislation. He had extensive executive power. And he had the huge moral force of being the only nationally elected official. As Paul Johnson writes in *A History of the American People,* the American president was "much stronger than most kings of the day." The strength alarmed King George's former subjects.

Washington perceived their fears. Though he was by nature an aristocrat, he recognized the nation's democratic essence. With great diligence and consideration for the competing interests of the young nation, he created a presidency sufficiently powerful for the needs of the moment.

R. Emmett Tyrrell, Jr.

Washington's prudence and restraint were ideal for the needs of the moment. They gave the young country the time it needed to realize the potential that some day would allow it to end two world wars on behalf of democracy.

Western front of Mount Vernon as it appeared in 1875.

GEORGE WILL

ESSAYIST, POLITICAL ANALYST, SYNDICATED COLUMNIST

"...he...walked away...."

George Will's twice-weekly column appears in nearly five hundred newspapers in the United States and Europe. He is a regular panelist on ABC Television's "This Week" and a contributing editor of *Newsweek*. A baseball aficionado and authority, he is the author of two books about the sport, as well as of six collections of essays and three books of political philosophy. A native of Illinois, he holds bachelor's degrees from Trinity College in Hartford and Magdalen College of Oxford University, England. He holds M.A. and Ph.D degrees from Princeton University.

Some see as paradoxical the idea that leaders should work to limit us. But George Washington's greatest claim to greatness—and he is, in my judgment, the great indispensable

American—is that he could have done anything for as long as he wished, yet he did less and walked away, thereby becoming an incarnation of the idea of leadership in a republic.

—From "Leadership," a lecture commemorating the twenty-fifth anniversary of the Heritage Foundation, in the Old State House, Hartford, Connecticut, January 28, 1999

Washington's book-plate.

BIBLIOGRAPHY

Adams, John. *Diary and Autobiography of John Adams.* L.H. Butterfield, ed. Cambridge, Massachusetts: The Belknap Press of Harvard University Press, 1961.

Bolle, Paul F., Jr. and George, John. *They Never Said it: A Book of False Quotes, Misquotes and Misleading Attributions.* New York: Oxford University Press, 1989.

Bowen, Catherine Drinker. *Miracle at Philadelphia.* Boston: Little, Brown and Company 1966.

Brookhiser, Richard. *Rediscovering George Washington.* New York: The Free Press, 1996.

Cunliffe, Marcus. *George Washington: Man and Monument.* Mount Vernon: Mount Vernon Ladies' Association, 1998.

Flexner, James Thomas. *Washington, The Indispensable Man.* New York: New American Library, 1974.

Freeman, Douglas Southall. *George Washington.* New York: Charles Scribner's Sons, 1949-57. (Volume Seven written following Freeman's death in 1953, by John Alexander Carroll and Mary Wells Ashworth.)

George Washington Bicentennial Commission (U.S.). *History of the George Washington Bicentennial Celebration.* Washington, D.C.: George Washington Bicentennial Commission (U.S.), 1932.

Jackman, S.W. "A Young Englishman reports on the New Nation." *William and Mary Quarterly*, January 1961.

Johnson, Paul. *History of the American People.* New York: HarperCollins, 1997.

Kaminski, John P. and McCaughan, Jill Adair, eds. *A Great and Good Man: George Washington in the Eyes of His Contemporaries*. Madison, Wisconsin: Madison House, 1989.

Kochman, Rachel M. *Presidents: Birthplaces, Homes and Burial Sites*. Detroit Lakes, Minnesota: Midwest Printing, 1976, 1990.

Lodge, Henry Cabot, Sr. *George Washington*. American Statesman Series. Boston: Houghton Mifflin and Company, 1889.

Lossing, Benson J. *Cyclopedia of the United States*. New York: Harper Brothers, 1888.

—. *Pictorial Field Book of the Revolution*. New York: Harper Brothers, 1859.

Perkins, Bradford. "A Diplomat's Wife in Philadelphia: Letters of Henrietta Liston, 1796-1800." *William and Mary Quarterly,* October 1954.

Schroeder, John Frederick (compiler). *Maxims of George Washington*. Mount Vernon: Mount Vernon Ladies' Association, 1989.

Spiller, Robert E. *Literary History of the United States*. New York: Macmillan, 1963.

Syrett, Harold C. ed. *The Papers of Alexander Hamilton*. New York: Columbia University Press, 1976.

Twohig, Dorothy ed. *The Papers of George Washington*. Charlottesville, Virginia: University Press of Virginia, 1996.

Wilson, Woodrow. *George Washington*. New York and London: Harper & Brothers Publishers, 1897, 1924.

CREDITS

IMAGES FROM THE PAST

Publishing history in ways that help people see it for themselves

Other of our books you might enjoy

WASHINGTON'S FAREWELL TO HIS OFFICERS:
After Victory in the Revolution
By Stuart Murray

In the sunlit Long Room of Fraunces Tavern, on a winter's day in New York City, 1783, George Washington's few remaining officers anxiously await his arrival. He has called them here to say goodbye-likely never to see them again. The British redcoats have sailed away, defeated in the Revolution. This moving incident, one almost forgotten in American history, was among the most telling and symbolic events of the War for Independence.

As they anticipate their beloved general's arrival, the officers recall how their struggle for the sacred cause flickered, almost went out, then flared into final victory. In the story of Washington's Farewell are the memories of long-struggling patriots—the famous and the little-known—men committed heart and soul to the cause of American liberty: Knox, McDougall, Lamb, Hamilton, Steuben, Shaw, Humphreys, Varick, Burnett, Hull, Fish, Tallmadge, the Clintons, Van Cortlandt, Fraunces...Heroes all. Index. Bibliography. 42 prints and maps.

5" x 7", 240 pages ISBN 10884592-20-1 Cloth $21.00

AMERICA'S SONG: The Story of Yankee Doodle
By Stuart Murray

During the first uncertain hours of the Revolution, British

redcoats sang "Yankee Doodle" as an insult to Americans - but when the rebels won astounding victories this song of insult was transformed to a song of triumph, eventually becoming "America's Song."

This is the first complete chronicle of the story of "Yankee Doodle," perhaps the best-known tune in all the world. From its early days an ancient air for dancing, through the era of Dutch and Puritan colonial settlement, "Yankee Doodle" evolved during the French and Indian Wars and the American Revolution to become our most stirring anthem of liberty. Index. Bibliography. Illustrated with 37 prints and maps. 5" x 7", 248 pages ISBN 1-884592-18-X Cloth $21.00

RUDYARD KIPLING IN VERMONT: Birthplace of The Jungle Books
By Stuart Murray

This book fills a gap in the biographical coverage of the important British author who is generally described as having lived only in India and England. It provides the missing links in the bitter-sweet story that haunts the portals of Naulakha, the distinctive shingle style home built by Kipling and his American wife near Brattleboro, Vermont. Here the Kiplings lived for four years and the first two of their three children were born.

All but one of Kipling's major works stem from these years of rising success, happiness and productivity; but because of a feud with his American brother-in-law, Beatty, which was seized on by newspaper reporters eager to put a British celebrity in his place, the author and his family left their home in America forever in 1896.

6"x9"; 208 pages; Extensive index. Excerpts from Kipling poems, 21 historical photos; 6 book illustrations; and 7 sketches convey the mood of the times, character of the peo-

ple, and style of Kipling's work.
ISBN 1-884592-04-X   Cloth $29.00   ISBN 1-884592-05-8
Paperback $18.95

THE HONOR OF COMMAND: Gen. Burgoyne's Saratoga Campaign
By Stuart Murray

Leaving Quebec in June, Burgoyne was confident in his ability to strike a decisive blow against the rebellion in the colonies. Instead, the stubborn rebels fought back, slowed his advance and inflicted irreplaceable losses, leading to his defeat and surrender at Saratoga on October 17, 1777—an important turning point in the American Revolution. Burgoyne's point of view as the campaign progresses is expressed from his dispatches, addresses to his army, and exchanges with friends and fellow officers.; 33 prints and engravings, 8 maps, 10 sketches. Index
7"x10", 128 pages ISBN 1-884-592-03-1 Paperback $14.95

NORMAN ROCKWELL AT HOME IN VERMONT: The Arlington Years, 1939-1953
By Stuart Murray

Norman Rockwell painted some of his greatest works, including "The Four Freedoms" during the 15 years he and his family lived in Arlington, Vermont. Compared to his former home in the suburbs of New York City, it was "like living in another world," and completely transformed his already successful career as America's leading illustrator. For the first time he began to paint pictures that "grew out of the every day life of my neighbors."
32 historical photographs, 13 Rockwell paintings and sketches, and personal recollections. Index. Regional map, select-

ed bibliography, and listing of area museums and exhibitions. 7"x10", 96 pages ISBN 1-884592-02-3 Paperback $14.95

LETTERS TO VERMONT Volumes I and II:
From Her Civil War Soldier Correspondents to the Home Press
Donald Wickman, Editor/Compiler

In their letters "To the Editor" of the Rutland Herald, young Vermont soldiers tell of fighting for the Union, galloping around Lee's army in Virginia, garrisoning the beleaguered defenses of Washington, D.C., and blunting Pickett's desperate charge at Gettysburg. One writer is captured, another serves as a prison camp guard, others are wounded—and one dies fighting in the horrific conflict in the Wilderness of Virginia. Biographical information for each writer (except one who remains an enigma) and supporting commentary on military affairs. 54 engravings and prints, 32 contemporary maps, 45 historical photographs. Extensive index.
Vol. 1, 6"x9", 251 pages ISBN 1-884592-10-4 Cloth $30.00
ISBN 1-884592-11-2 Paper $19.95
Vol. 2, 6"x9", 265 pages ISBN 1-884592-16-3 Cloth $30.00
ISBN 1-884592-17-1 Paper $19.95

ALLIGATORS ALWAYS DRESS FOR DINNER: An
Alphabet Book of Vintage Photographs
By Linda Donigan and Michael Horwitz

A collection of late 19th- and early 20th-century images from around the world reproduced in rich duo tone for children and all who love historical pictures. Each two-page spread offers a surprising visual treat: Beholding Beauty—a beautifully dressed and adorned Kikuyu couple; Fluted Fingers—a wandering Japanese Zen monk playing a bamboo recorder;

and Working the Bandwagon—the Cole Brothers Band on an elaborate 1879 circus wagon. A-Z information pages with image details.
9 1/4"x9 3/4", 64 pages ISBN 1-884592-08-2 Cloth $25.00

REMEMBERING GRANDMA MOSES
By Beth Moses Hickok

Grandma Moses, a crusty, feisty, upstate New York farm wife and grandmother, as remembered in affectionate detail by Beth Moses Hickok, who married into the family at 22, and raised two of Grandma's granddaughters. Set in 1934, before the artist was "discovered", the book includes family snapshots, and photographs that evoke the landscape of Eagle Bridge, home for most of her century-plus life. Two portraits of Grandma Moses—a 1947 painting and a 1949 photograph, and nine historical photographs. On the cover is a rare colorful yarn painting given to the author as a wedding present.
6" x 9", 64 pages ISBN 1-884592-01-5 Paperback $12.95

REMAINS UNKNOWN
By Michael J. Caduto with sixteen pencil sketches by Adelaide Murphy Tyrol

He somehow found his way to Vermont soon after the Mexican War. It was a long journey, the beginning of a private purgatory that lasted over 150 years. At last, with the help of friends he'd never met, he took the final steps in a quiet cemetery by the river on a sultry afternoon.
In this strange and haunting tale, based on a true story, the reader enters a world suspended between our earthly existence and the realm of the human spirit. A small community of people embarks on an adventure that compels them to

bring the mysterious, mummified remains of one long dead to a resting place of peace and grace. With help from two distinct spiritual traditions, and a dose of healing humor in the face of grief, the journey unfolds with a sense of dignity and compassion.

5"x7", 80 pages ISBN 1-884592-24-4 Cloth $15.00

Available at your local bookstore or from Images from the Past, Inc., 888-4423204 for credit card orders; P.O. Box 137, Bennington, Vermont 05201 with check or money order. When ordering, please add $4.00 shipping and handling for the first book and $1 for each additional. (Add 5% sales tax for shipments to Vermont.) www.ImagesfromthePast.com